Ed Weeks is a solicitor and head of the commercial dispute resolution team at Cripps LLP. He has been resolving shareholder disputes for over 20 years and is recognised as an expert in this field. Family businesses are particularly susceptible to such disputes and he has gained particular expertise and insight in how to approach such disputes and the specific issues that arise.

A Practical Guide to Shareholder Disputes in Family Businesses

A Practical Guide to Shareholder Disputes in Family Businesses

Ed Weeks
Solicitor

Law Brief Publishing

Published 2021 by Law Brief Publishing, an imprint of Law Brief Publishing Ltd
30 The Parks
Minehead
Somerset
TA24 8BT

www.lawbriefpublishing.com

Paperback: 978-1-913715-47-2

My thanks go to Anna, Eva, Eliza and Hal for allowing me the time and space to write this book.

Thanks also to my colleague Jo Ford for taking the time to read it and giving me her thoughts on the structure.

PREFACE

This book is the product of over 20 years of resolving disputes in family businesses. It is intended to help those who find themselves involved in such disputes, whether as a legal or other adviser to the business or as a director or shareholder in the business.

It is not intended to be technical discourse on the underlying law but instead an overall guide to the legal, practical and commercial issues that need to be considered in understanding and resolving these disputes.

Some chapters may well be a case of teaching grandma to suck eggs for more seasoned legal practitioners but will, I hope, at least provide some suggestions of new ways to explain things to the lay person.

The law stated is correct and up-to-date as at 31 January 2021.

Ed Weeks
February 2021

CONTENTS

Chapter One	Introduction What makes family businesses different? Types of disputes and dispute resolution mechanisms	1
Chapter Two	Corporate Governance – The Documentation What to look out for in terms of documentation including articles of association, shareholders' agreements and family charters	7
Chapter Three	Corporate Governance – Rights and Duties What are the rights and duties of directors and shareholders? What is the key legislation?	13
Chapter Four	Gathering the Evidence The relative importance of documentary evidence and witness evidence	27
Chapter Five	Unfair Prejudice A look at the application of s.994 / s.996 of the Companies Act 2006	31
Chapter Six	Winding Up Winding up under s.122(1)(g) of the Insolvency Act 1996 and Voluntary Liquidation	45
Chapter Seven	Other Claims Under the Companies Act Derivative claims and rectification applications	53

Chapter Eight Alternative Dispute Resolution and Settlement 57

Offers of settlement (including O'Neill offers), mediating family business disputes and the role of expert determination

Chapter Nine Advising Majority Shareholders 69

Key legal and commercial points

Chapter Ten Advising Minority Shareholders 77

Key legal and commercial points (including funding shareholder litigation)

Chapter Eleven Deceased Shareholders and Bankrupt Shareholders 83

Dealing with issues affecting the transmission of shares

Chapter Twelve Valuing the Company / Shareholding 87

Key points on valuation from a legal perspective

Chapter Thirteen The Litigation Process 97

Practical points in relation to the process of litigating shareholder disputes

Chapter Fourteen Case Studies 105

Some examples of judicial thinking and cautionary tales from reported cases

Chapter Fifteen Conclusions 117

Key steps to resolving shareholder disputes in family businesses

CHAPTER ONE

INTRODUCTION

All businesses are ultimately defined by the people who work in them. What makes family businesses different are the ties between members which extend beyond the typical commercial and business relationships.

This can make resolving disputes between the members of the business more difficult and also has an impact on the legal and practical issues that can arise.

This book is written from a lawyer's perspective and hence the focus is on the law. However there are three elements which are relevant to understanding family business disputes and which are equally important:

- Law
- Psychology
- Commercial context

Anybody tasked with resolving such a dispute must understand the interaction between these three elements and in particular must never underestimate the importance of the psychology of those involved.

In the words of the author F. Scott Fitzgerald:

> "*Family quarrels are bitter things. They don't go according to any rules. They're not like aches or wounds, they're more like splits in the skin that won't heal because there's not enough material.*"

There are also a number of practical differences between family companies and non-family companies. Those which are relevant to the likelihood of disputes and to the approach which may need to be taken to achieve resolution include the following:

- There are more likely to be understandings and agreements outside of the formal company structure or governing documents.

- It is more likely that shareholders will have an elevated sense of ownership and expectations about their entitlements.

- There is greater potential for directors or employees to have been appointed to roles above their capabilities.

- From a technical legal perspective such companies are more likely to be what have become known in legal shorthand as "quasi-partnerships".

- Issues around succession can either be the direct cause of disputes or be a contributing factor, heightening emotion and ill-feeling between the parties.

These elements, and the issues and elephant traps that arise from them, will be explored further in the following chapters.

The causes and nature of disputes within family businesses are as many and varied as the businesses themselves but there are some common themes:

- Disagreements over the direction of the business, in particular whether it should be seen as a long-term income generator as opposed to there being a planned exit route to realising the capital in the business by sale in the short to medium term.

- People not pulling their weight. Sometimes this can relate to a shareholder appointed to a role beyond their capability but more often it is the result of shares being left on death by a parent to all siblings, regardless of whether they take an active role in the business. Resentment can build in those actively involved in the business when they feel they are doing all the work but having to share the reward.

- People feathering their own nest. This is the reverse of the previous theme in that the non-active shareholders believe that those controlling the company are preferring their own interests over the company and the wider group of shareholders.

- Inter-generational conflict. This can occur where the shares are held by different generations who have different priorities and consequently different expectations about the future of the business.

- Sibling rivalry, plain and simple. Sometimes the cause of a dispute has its roots in childhood rivalries that re-emerge or have never gone away. These can be some of the hardest disputes for a lawyer to resolve.

The nature and cause of the underlying dispute should be sought to be understood at the earliest possible stage as it has an impact on the appropriate dispute mechanism and the ultimate chances of that mechanism being successful in resolving the dispute.

In terms of mechanisms the principal ones are, in ascending order of complexity and cost:

- Informal discussion and negotiation

- Facilitated negotiation

- Mediation

- Expert determination

- Litigation / Arbitration

In terms of selecting an appropriate dispute resolution mechanism, those tasked with resolving a dispute should first identify the stage which the conflict has reached. Friedrich Glasl, an Austrian economist and leading authority on conflict, has created a model which identifies three main stages as follows:

- Win-Win – the parties are engaging, disputes are mostly factual and negotiation, facilitated or otherwise, is the right mechanism.

- Win-Lose – positions have become entrenched, attacks are more personal and the conflict is more about the relationship. At this stage a more structured negotiation (e.g. mediation) is likely to be required.

- Lose-Lose – it has reached the stage where parties are using the language of war, are willing to incur losses as long as their opponent loses more or even are ready to destroy their own position to take down their opponent. When it has reached this stage it is likely that only the intervention of a third party making a decision (i.e. Judge), or at least the credible threat of this, will lead to any resolution.

In family businesses the nature of the relationships between the parties can often mean that there can be an accelerated progress through the stages, disputes quickly moving into the lose-lose phase. For this reason early intervention in any dispute is always preferable.

Informal discussion and negotiation should always be explored at the outset of any dispute. It can be the case that there are misunderstandings or miscommunications which can be cleared up by frank and open discussions between the parties. Often a trusted adviser, such as a lawyer, accountant or even family friend can be brought in to facilitate the discussions and chair a meeting. Occasionally such discussions can do more harm than good but in most cases they have merely exposed a rift which could not be bridged in any event and have therefore just accelerated the inevitable.

If the conflict has escalated then mediation is a powerful tool to find a resolution and this is discussed in more detail in chapter 8. It should be noted that mediation can be deployed at any time but generally the earlier the better.

If the parties are at war then the binding decision of a third party may be the only outcome that can achieve a resolution. In some circumstances an expert determination may be appropriate (considered in more detail in chapter 8) otherwise it may be necessary to seek the ruling of a Judge or an Arbitrator.

Arbitration is a private dispute resolution process under which the parties present their case and an Arbitrator takes on the role of the Judge. An Arbitrator will make an Award, rather than a Judgment, and this is contractually binding on the parties. An Arbitrator can only be appointed if there is an agreement between the parties to this effect. Sometimes arbitration clauses can be found in shareholder agreements but this is relatively rare. Given this, and the fact that most arbitrations will mirror litigation in terms of the basic process leading up to the hearing of the parties' respective cases, this book will focus on the litigation (i.e. court) process.

With regard to shareholder dispute litigation the main legal actions that can be taken are:

- Petition for unfair prejudice under s.994 of the Companies Act 2006 (s.994)

- Petition for just and equitable winding up under s.122(1)(g) of the Insolvency Act 1996 (s.122(1)(g))

- A derivative action (one brought by a shareholder but on behalf of the company)

- An application for rectification

These are considered in more detail in the following chapters.

CHAPTER TWO

CORPORATE GOVERNANCE – THE DOCUMENTATION

All shareholder disputes must be seen in the context of the underlying corporate governance documents.

Disputes can arise because directors or shareholders are:

- breaching the provisions of the documentation or are exceeding their powers; or
- exercising their rights or powers in an unfair way.

In the former case the wrong suffered is easier to identify and the remedy consequently more straightforward to pursue.

The relevant formal documentation likely to be encountered in family companies may include the following:

- Memorandum and Articles of Association
- Shareholders' agreements
- Family Charters / Family Constitutions

However, the informal nature of many family business structures may mean that the formal documentation is actually very limited, perhaps no more than an "off the shelf" set of Articles of Association.

This is more likely to be the case in a family business which is the subject of a dispute that ends up in the hands of lawyers as standard Articles of Association lack any dispute resolution mechanism or other useful provisions which can nip such a dispute in the bud.

Articles of Association

Every company must have Articles of Association. They regulate the company's internal affairs and are effectively a contract between the members (i.e. shareholders) of the company. Section 33(1) of the Companies Act 2006 provides that:

> "*The provisions of a company's constitution bind the company and its members to the same extent as if there were covenants on the part of the company and of each member to observe those provisions.*"

A key difference between the contract created by the Articles of Association and other commercial contracts is that where the latter requires unanimous consent to change its terms, Articles of Association can be changed via majority vote of 75% or more of those eligible (a special resolution). In addition, Articles of Association must have regard to sections in the Companies Act which prohibit certain provisions or impose specific requirements. One such example is s.168(1) of the Companies Act 2006 which provides that a director may be removed from office by an ordinary resolution notwithstanding anything in the Articles of Association.

The Companies Act 2006 and its predecessors provide default models for Articles of Association which can simply be adopted without amendment or be subject to certain changes to cover the specific requirements of any individual company.

Before 1 October 2009 this was known as 'Table A' with versions being created as far back 1856. After 1 October 2009 a new version was created, renamed the 'Model Articles'.

The first step is to ascertain which edition of Table A or Model Articles applies and whether it has been amended. A certain amount of due diligence is required in this respect as the impressively bound hard copy handed over by a shareholder can often have been superseded by a new version put in place as the result of changes in the law or company structure.

All Articles of Association should cover the following essential matters:

- The rights and liabilities of shareholders
- The powers and responsibilities of directors
- Decision making by directors and shareholders
- Share rights, transfers and distributions
- Administrative arrangements

Those acting for either side in any dispute need to review the document to ascertain whether there has been a breach of the Articles of Association or whether it is a case of legitimate rights being used for illegitimate purposes.

In the former case there may be remedies within the Articles of Association themselves. Otherwise, if a shareholder's personal rights under the Articles of Association are being infringed then they will be entitled to bring a claim in their personal capacity to enforce those rights. This includes the ability to seek a court order declaring a particular step null and void or obtaining an injunction to prevent a particular step being taken.

However, more often it is the latter case, one party acting within their strict legal rights under the Articles of Association, but to the unfair detriment of another. This will require a different approach.

Shareholders' agreement

In addition to the formal Articles of Association some owner managed businesses will have a separate shareholders' agreement. This is a bespoke agreement made between all shareholders intended to govern how the company will operate. It will do this by, for example:

- Giving rights to individual shareholders to appoint or remove directors;
- Regulating the power of directors or embedding a particular shareholder as a director;

- Requiring that certain decisions or steps will require the approval of a majority (or even all) of the shareholders;

- Providing exit mechanisms for shareholders who wish to leave;

- Providing compulsory share transfer provisions which apply in certain defined circumstances;

- Implementing a dispute resolution process in the event of a breakdown in relations.

Such matters can also be included in a bespoke set of Articles of Association but for various reasons are more usually found in a separate (and private) shareholders' agreement.

Those specialising in dispute resolution, particularly in the context of family businesses, may rarely come across a well drafted shareholders' agreement. The reasons for this being twofold. First, such a document can prevent disputes arising or provide a mechanism such that lawyers are not required to be involved. Secondly, family businesses will often not see the need for such an agreement as they are run on the basis of trust and personal relationships. Rather like a pre-nuptial agreement in a personal relationship being seen as unromantic, a shareholders' agreement can be seen as an unduly pessimistic assessment of family relationships and consequently unnecessary.

If there is a shareholders' agreement then its terms need to be examined carefully to see whether there are any mechanisms that can be deployed in the circumstances or whether there are any breaches of its terms. Such a breach is a breach of contract, with the consequent remedies that can be deployed in this respect, but may also amount to an act of unfairly prejudicial conduct (a concept explored in more detail in chapter 5).

Family Charters / Family Constitutions

These are less formal documents which set out, often in non-legal terms, how a business is intended to be run and how shareholder / director relationships are intended to work. They are not common but if one exists it can provide a valuable guide to the wider understandings within a family business which may be relevant to determining whether any specific action, although not in breach of any power or rule, may nevertheless be a breach of somebody's legitimate expectations (another concept which is explored in more detail later in the book).

Other documents

The early collation of all key background documents (emails, letters, minutes, notes of meetings etc) is vital to establish the factual position underlying any family business dispute. The importance of this exercise is analysed in more detail in chapter 4.

CHAPTER THREE

CORPORATE GOVERNANCE – RIGHTS AND DUTIES

Members of family companies often wear three hats – those of shareholder, director and employee. It is not always straightforward in family businesses to identify which hat a party is wearing in the context of any particular action and there is often a blurring of lines between the different roles.

As an employee they have a raft of rights which are outside the scope of this book. For current purposes it should be noted that employment tribunal proceedings may run in parallel to any other litigation arising from a family business dispute and the fact of dismissal as an employee may form the basis of a separate claim for unfair prejudice (see below).

The focus in this book is on the roles of director and shareholder. The role of director brings with it a number of powerful rights and also responsibilities. As a shareholder there are fewer rights and fewer responsibilities, but ultimately control of the company (by simple majority) vests with them.

The legal nature of companies

A company is a separate legal entity, distinct from its directors and shareholders. This means, amongst other things, that a company may sue, or be sued by, its directors and/or shareholders. In many cases the company is the only possible claimant in relation to wrongdoing that has occurred, for example a breach of fiduciary duty by one of its directors.

This is an important principle that is often not understood by shareholders. They may assume that if a director does something wrong then they as a shareholder in the company will have a direct right to go to court to seek a remedy. Under a principle originating in a historic case and known as the rule in Foss v Harbottle it is firmly established that where an actionable wrong has been done to a company the company is the proper claimant. Whilst there have been dissenting judicial views in modern cases the principle remains intact as far as most shareholders are concerned. In other words, in legal parlance, a shareholder has no cause of action. The derivative action (see chapter 7) was devised by the court to provide a remedy in this situation but it is an imperfect one.

Accordingly, a key question in relation to understanding any shareholders dispute is always – who controls the company?

The key document which sets out the balance of power within a company is the Articles of Association of the company ('the Articles'). Subject to any overriding company law the Articles determine who within a company exercises which powers on its behalf.

The rights of directors

The directors generally control the business and assets of a company on a day-to-day basis. This means the right to make decisions for the company including whether or not to enter into any contract, or to raise finance or take any other steps in relation to the management of the company.

In broad summary, all power lies with them unless something has been specifically reserved to the shareholders of the company under the Companies Act 2006 (see the table below) in the Articles or in a shareholders' agreement.

Generally the board of directors must act as a majority and subject to any quorum specified in the Articles any decision simply requires a majority vote.

This means that the status of director in a family business is very important. The board of directors can take significant decisions such as the sale of business assets without reference to shareholders. A shareholder vote about such issues is not effective to directly bind the directors unless the Articles say different.

A key right of directors is to information and documentation about the business. Unlike shareholders, whose rights are limited in this respect, directors are generally entitled to see all company documentation and information. This is a matter of common law but is not without its limits. The Judge in the case of *Re. Westshield Ltd [2019] EWHC 115 (Ch)* at paragraph 130 of the judgment puts it as follows:

> *"It is right that a director as director is entitled to the information necessary to enable him or her properly to undertake the duties of a director. It is also right that a company's board as board is entitled to full information about every aspect of a company's affairs. That does not, however, mean that a director is simply by virtue of his position as director entitled to see all e-mails or other documents generated in the course of the company's business. In particular there can be circumstances where a managing director or board chairman needs to deal with matters confidentially from another director or has conduct of matters with which another director has no reason to be concerned. There can be no confidentiality from the board of a company acting as the board but that does not mean that a director is, without board approval, entitled to see every document which a company has."*

Given that knowledge is power, the rights of access to information and documentation relating to a company can be key battleground in any internal company dispute. A single director on a board has valuable rights, but they can ultimately be trumped by a board majority.

The duties of directors

Directors have fiduciary and statutory duties that are owed to the company for which they act.

Fiduciary duties arise from common law and reflect the fact that a director does not (directly) own the company assets and is controlling them and exercising their powers for the company's benefit such that they are in effect a trustee of those assets.

The statutory duties are contained in chapter 2 of Part 10 of the Companies Act 2006 and can be summarised as follows:

s.171 – to act within their powers:

A director must act in accordance with their company's constitution (i.e. the company's Articles of Association);

s.172 – to promote the success of the company for the member's benefit:

A director must act in the way he or she considers, in good faith, would be most likely to promote the success of the company for the benefit of its members as a whole. In order to meet this obligation, a director must have regard (amongst other matters) to:

a) the likely consequences of any decision in the long term;

b) the interests of the company's employees;

c) the need to foster the company's business relationships with suppliers, customers and others;

d) the impact of the company's operations on the community and the environment;

e) the desirability of the company maintaining a reputation for high standards of business conduct; and

f) the need to act fairly as between the members of the company.

s.173 – to exercise independent judgment:

This is a general duty but is not infringed by a director acting (a) in accordance with an agreement entered into by the company that restricts the future exercise of the directors' discretion or (b) in a way authorised by the company's constitution.

s.174 – to exercise reasonable care, skill and diligence:

A director must exercise the care, skill and diligence which would be exercised by a reasonably diligent person with both the general knowledge, skill and experience that may be reasonably expected of a person carrying out the functions carried out by the director in relation to the company and the general knowledge, skill and experience that the director actually has.

This has been interpreted to include the following duties (also found at common law):

- to obey lawful instructions from the company;
- to display such reasonable care in the carrying out of responsibilities as an ordinary prudent person might be expected to take in the same circumstances;
- to carry out responsibilities personally (unless authorised to delegate them); and
- to act at all times in good faith.

s.175 – to avoid conflicts of interest:

This is a duty to avoid conflicts of interest between personal interests and the interests of the company.

It applies in particular to the exploitation of any property, information or opportunity (and it is immaterial whether the company could take advantage of the property, information or opportunity).

s.176 – not to accept benefits from third parties:

Directors must not accept any benefit (such as an incentive or bribe) from a third party which is conferred because of their role as director or in relation to them doing or not doing something as a director.

s.177 – to declare an interest in a proposed transaction or arrangement with the company:

A director must not make a secret or illegal profit from property, assets or opportunities which are properly the company's. Directors must declare to the other directors the *nature* and *extent* of any interest, direct or indirect in a proposed transaction or arrangement with the company. The director need not be a party to the transaction for the duty to apply. An interest of another person in a contract with the company may require the director to make a disclosure under this duty, if the other person's interest amounts to a direct or indirect interest on the part of the director. Such declarations must be made before the company enters into the transaction or arrangement.

As stated above, the duties in sections 171 to 177 of the Companies Act 2006 are owed collectively to the company. In ordinary trading circumstances (where there is no question-mark over the solvency or financial position of the company), this is generally interpreted as meaning that directors must act in the best interests of the company's shareholders.

The duties are owed by all directors, regardless of the role they play and the basis of their holding office.

The key point to emphasise is that these duties are owed to the company not the shareholders themselves. Shareholders do have a route to take action on behalf of the company if they believe that the directors of the company are in breach of their duties, known as a derivative action, but in practice this does not always provide a useful remedy (see chapter 7).

The rights of shareholders

Although directors have the day-to-day control of the company, shareholders (in theory at least) hold the ultimate power. By majority vote shareholders can dismiss directors and can appoint new directors to the board (although the latter power is often restricted by the Articles or in a shareholders' agreement).

By taking control of the board of directors a shareholder will then be able to force the company to take a desired course of action (which might include a claim by the company against a director guilty of some wrongdoing).

However, this ultimate power does not assist an unhappy shareholder where they are a minority shareholder. In that case the shareholder must rely upon one of the remedies below if the majority shareholders are in control of the company via the directors.

All shareholders, whatever the size of their shareholding, have certain rights. These include the right to ask the court to call a general meeting and to receive notice of any general meeting and vote at the meeting, the right to inspect minutes of general meetings and the register of members and the right not to be unfairly prejudiced.

With a 5% shareholding, shareholders have a right to call a general meeting and to require the circulation of a written statement in this respect.

With a 10% holding shareholders have the right to have the company's annual accounts audited, at the company's expense.

Over 25% means that a shareholder can block a special resolution. Such resolutions are required, for example, to amend a company's Articles.

What these powers do is give minority shareholders some leverage which can be deployed in the event of a dispute with other shareholders / directors. In any event these rights should not be forgotten as the court will give short shrift to a claim that a minority shareholder has been unfairly prejudiced if they have failed to take proper advantage of their statutory rights under the Companies Act 2006.

Below is a table setting out the key rights of shareholders under the Companies Act 2006:

Section	Effect	Notes
21	A right to amend articles of association (by special resolution)	Not less than 75% of vote
32	A right to be supplied with copies of constitutional documents	Any shareholder

116	A right to inspect the register of members (without charge) and obtain a copy	Any shareholder
162	A right to inspect the register of directors (without charge)	Any shareholder
168	Ordinary resolution enough to remove a director from office	Simple majority (special notice)
188	Approval needs to be obtained from members for directors' long term service contracts	Simple majority
190	Approval needs to be obtained from members for substantial property transactions between the company and any director	Simple majority
197	Approval needs to be obtained from members for loans to directors	Simple majority See also 198, 200, 201 & 203
217	Approval needs to be obtained from members for payments to directors for loss of office	Simple majority See also 218 & 219
229	A right to inspect a copy of the terms of directors' service agreements	Any shareholder
238	A right to inspect a copy of the terms of directors' indemnity provisions	Any shareholder

239	Approval needs to be obtained from members for the ratification by the company of any acts of directors in breach of duty etc	Simple majority
260	A right to bring proceedings on behalf of the company against a defaulting director	Known as a "derivative action"
275	A right to inspect the register of secretaries (without charge)	Any shareholder
291	A right to receive a copy of any written resolution proposed by directors	Any shareholder
292	A right to require the company to circulate a written resolution	Requires at least 5% holding
293	A right to receive a copy of any written resolution proposed by members	Any shareholder
303	A right to require the directors to call a general meeting	Requires at least 10% / 5% holding
310	A right to receive notice of general meetings	Any shareholder
314	A right to require the company to circulate a statement in relation to any general meeting	Requires at least 5% holding
321	A right to demand a poll vote	Requires at least 10% holding

324	A right to appoint a proxy to vote at general meetings	Any shareholder
358	A right to inspect records of shareholder resolutions and minutes of general meetings (without charge)	Any shareholder
366	Approval needs to be obtained from members for donations to political parties	Simple majority
423	A right to receive a copy of the company's annual accounts / reports when circulated generally	Any shareholder
431	A right to be supplied with a copy of the company's annual accounts / reports on request (without charge)	Any shareholder
476	A right to require audited accounts	Requires at least 10% holding
488	A right to object to deemed re-appointment of auditors	Requires at least 5% holding
510	Ordinary resolution sufficient to remove an auditor from office	Simple majority (special notice)
551	Ordinary resolution required to authorise directors to allot shares (where not already authorised to do so by articles)	Simple majority

561	Pre-emption rights on allotment of shares (can be excluded in Articles)	See also 561 to 577
630	Special resolution required to vary class rights	Not less than 75% of vote
693 / 701	Approval of purchase of companies own shares must be given by the members	
633	Right to object to variation of class rights	Requires at least 15% holding
744	Right to inspect and receive copies of the register of holders of debentures	Any shareholder
983	Right of minority shareholder to be bought out by offeror on a takeover	See Part 28 of the Companies Act 2006 for the wider context
994	Right to petition in relation to unfair prejudice	Any shareholder

Some of these rights can be usefully employed in the context of a family business disputes, for example:

- A director can be removed from office by simple majority (unless they have been embedded by, for example, weighted voting rights);

- The right to call a general meeting can be deployed as a mechanism to get parties around the table and ventilate any issues (although note that members cannot generally use shareholder votes at such meetings to bind the board of directors);

- The right to seek audited accounts can be of real nuisance value in those companies which take a more relaxed approach to accounting / taxation issues. It should however be noted that the right must be exercised at least one month prior to the end of the accounting period in question and there is no retrospective right to seek an audit. Furthermore, the shareholders can do no more than require the accounts to be audited, they have no right to choose the auditor or direct them to carry out any investigations. However, whilst shareholders have no right to any direct input into the auditor's instructions, if there are significant matters of concern these can be communicated to the auditors who may be under a professional obligation to at the very least raise the issue with the directors, although not obliged to share with shareholders the details of any discussions in this respect.

Shareholders also have some personal rights under common law. These include:

- the right to enforce rights as members conferred by the Articles (for example where the directors act or propose to act contrary to the Articles),

- the right to object to an improper alteration of the Articles,

- the right to bring an action to prevent a proposed ultra vires transaction (i.e. a transaction that is outside the power of the company or its directors).

It should be noted that there are limits to what loss can be recovered by shareholders in personal claims if the company itself has a parallel cause of action. In such cases a shareholder cannot recover losses which are effectively reflective of the loss which has been suffered by the company ('the no reflective loss principle"). An example of such loss is the diminution in value of a shareholding (where this is pro rata to a diminution in value of the entire shareholding). This is considered to be reflective loss which may not be recovered. This is a complex area of law and therefore careful consideration needs to be given to the merits of any case where these circumstances apply.

If there is a shareholders' agreement in place then the shareholder may also have remedies under this which are enforceable against the signatories of the agreement in the same way as any other contract. Note in this respect that the company itself may be a party to a shareholders' agreement and in such circumstances a shareholder may have a remedy against the company itself as well as against other shareholder parties.

The duties of shareholders

Shareholders do not owe duties to the company in the way that a director does. In voting they are generally entitled to prefer their own interests without regard to other factors.

Shareholders control the company by simple majority voting (except where modified as for example is shown in the table above). This means the majority rule and can act to prefer their own interests over those of minority shareholders. However, minority shareholders are given statutory protection in this respect from "unfair prejudice" (see chapter 5).

CHAPTER FOUR

GATHERING THE EVIDENCE

The nature of family businesses means that many transactions are not documented properly or at all and there may not be formal board minutes or even board meetings as such. Litigation in relation to family businesses can therefore be heavily reliant on oral witness evidence. In these circumstances there is a reliance upon the recollections and memories of witnesses. In a family business dispute, where more may be perceived to be at stake for parties than in a purely commercial relationship, there may be a greater likelihood for recollections, either consciously or unconsciously, to be adjusted by parties to reflect their preferred narrative of events.

As a result, there can often be a disconnect between the contents of witness statements and what ultimately emerges in evidence at trial when such evidence is tested in cross-examination.

There is a particular danger that witness statements get "over-lawyered", a problem recognised by the Witness Evidence Working Group in their report on the use of witness evidence in trials before the Business & Property Courts which was published in December 2019. They identified the risk that a written witness statement ends up not being the unvarnished own words of the witness but rather the product of a long process of drafting and polishing by the lawyers to promote a particular version of the truth.

Judges are alive to this issue, and as will be seen from some of the cases highlighted in this book, often treat witness evidence as to facts in a very sceptical way. What this means is that the strength of any case can be dependent upon what ancillary contemporaneous documents there are which tend to support the existence of a set of facts. For example, a Judge faced with two opposing accounts of an oral agreement will look to find any documentary evidence which will assist in establishing the truth.

A key task of a lawyer engaged in a shareholder dispute in a family business is to collate every document that might have a bearing on the key facts. There is a need to think laterally. For example, in relation to an oral agreement, are there emails before or after which indicate a direction of travel or show the terms alleged being actually applied. Are there calendar or diary entries confirming a meeting took place? Is there a provable fact as to something which has or has not happened which is indicative of such an agreement being in place?

The importance of such evidence and the risks of relying on oral witness evidence was flagged up in the case of *Northampton Borough Council v Cardoza [2019] EWHC26 (Ch).*

This was a case involving a family business, a football club, and the expropriation of funds from the company. The judgment in the case was scathing about the evidence given by the defendant directors and the reliance that could be placed it on it.

The Judge, HHJ Simon Barker QC described the first defendant, the father, as follows:

> *"D1's demeanour as a witness was urbane and engaging. However, his demeanour is a front for a person who, at least in business and in litigation, is thoroughly untrustworthy and unreliable."*

His description of the second defendant, the son, was equally damning:

> *"D2 is proud to be viewed as a man in his father's image. He readily admitted that, like his father, he believes that lying and suppressing the truth is part and parcel of doing business."*

In relation to both the Judge summarised as follows:

> *"My conclusion is that truth is a concept of no value or significance to D2, even when on oath. As with D1, unless consistent with undisputed facts or supported by independent documents, D2's evidence was, and is to be viewed as, unreliable."*

The Judge also cited with approval a passage from the judgment of Leggatt J in the case of *Gestmin SGPSA SA v Credit Suisse (UK) Limited [2013] EWHC 3560* which he summarised as follows:

> *"After noting that human memory is fallible and that the process of litigation and preparing for trial tends to interfere further with the reliability of human memory, particularly where a lawyer has had a hand in drafting a witness's evidence and the witness's memory has been refreshed by reading documents, Leggatt J concluded that the best approach for a judge to adopt at the trial of a commercial case is to base factual findings on documentary evidence and known or probable facts and the inferences to be drawn therefrom. Witness evidence, written and oral, is not without purpose; but, its principal uses are to subject the documentary record to scrutiny and to evaluate the witness's motivations, personality and working practices."*

What this indicates is that the courts will always strive to base factual findings on proven facts and documentary evidence, and witness evidence (whether oral or written) will be regarded and relied upon only with a great deal of caution.

As Leggatt J put it in the Gestmin case:

> *"it is important to avoid the fallacy of supposing that, because a witness has confidence in his or her recollection and is honest, evidence based on that recollection provides any reliable guide to the truth"*

Lawyers must therefore be alive to the fact that human memory is fallible and recollections of witnesses can be distorted by the litigation process (saying what they think a lawyer wants to hear) and this can be the case even for honest witnesses. It is therefore a high-risk strategy to rely upon oral evidence alone in family business disputes, as is illustrated by some of the case examples given later.

CHAPTER FIVE

UNFAIR PREJUDICE

As noted in chapter 3, the principle of "majority rule" applies at both a board of directors and shareholder level. This means that if majority shareholders stay within their rights as set out in the Articles of Association then on the face of it a minority shareholder has no remedy for a majority decision that adversely affects them.

However, since the Companies Act 1948 there has been statutory protection for minority shareholders against oppressive conduct by a majority. More recently the remedy was found in s.459 of the Companies Act 1985 (hence references in some of the cases cited to "s.459 petitions"). The protection can now be found in sections 994 – 996 of the Companies Act 2006 (although it is essentially the same as in previous acts and therefore the historic case law is still of relevance).

The role of this legislation was summarised by Patten LJ in *Re Fulham Football Club (1987) Ltd CH 333 [57]* as follows:

> *"The remedy to deal with unfair prejudice introduced by s.210 of the Companies Act 1948 and now contained in section 994 like the court's use of its jurisdiction under s.122(1)(g) to wind up companies formed on the basis of a quasi-partnership was designed to deal with disputes between members of private companies (usually minority shareholders) who may be the subject of oppression but are prevented by the articles or a shareholders' agreement from taking effective steps to resolve their difficulties or to realise the value of their investment in the company by a sale of their shares."*

It is useful to look at some of the wording from this quote in a little more detail with reference to disputes in family businesses.

What is meant by "unfair prejudice" is considered in detail below but the key point to understand in this context is that the concept of what is unfair has been addressed in many cases over many years with the judicial intention being to introduce as much objectivity as possible into what might otherwise be a subjective process. Thus, merely because something is unfair in a family context does not make it unfair for the purposes of s.994.

This concept was described by Lord Hoffman in the leading case of *Re. Guidezone Limited [2000] 2 BCLC 321*, referring back to the pivotal case of *O'Neill v Phillips [1999] 2 BCLC 1* as follows:

> *"... "unfairness" for the purposes of s.459 [the predecessor of s.994] is not to be judged by reference to subjective notions of fairness, but rather by testing whether, applying established equitable principles, the majority has acted, or is proposing to act, in a manner which equity would regard as contrary to good faith."*

Thus it can be seen that one critical component of unfairness is bad faith. Whilst it is not essential to prove bad faith, actions that are taken by the majority in bad faith are highly likely to be found to be unfair.

The concept of "quasi-partnership" is an important one and it is often the case that the family businesses fall into this category. This can be critical to whether or not a remedy is available and also the nature of that remedy. This is considered in more detail below.

The protection provided by s.994 is only available to members (i.e. shareholders) in the company, although this includes those who are entitled to be shareholders by operation of law (i.e. executors of a deceased shareholder and/or the beneficiaries of the shares). Claims to some other entitlement to a shareholding give rise to a different cause of action outside of s.994.

The protection is primarily aimed at minority shareholders, but can also be sought by majority shareholders in circumstances where minority shareholders are abusing their rights. This is very rare but an example might be the refusal of minority shareholders holding in excess of 25% of the shares to agree to a special resolution when there is a legitimate expectation that it would be agreed to.

An important concept is that of "oppression". This is a key ingredient of what makes what would otherwise be a lawful exercise of rights "unfairly prejudicial" such that s.994 can be brought into play. What is oppressive will depend upon the facts of each case. This must be looked at in the context of all the available facts and from both sides. One trap which advisers can fall into is the failure to see the opposing point of view. An uncritical approach to their own client's case may result in the failure to identify facts which make apparently unfair actions justified in the circumstances.

The purpose of the remedy can be described as to enable those who are unfairly prejudiced to "resolve their difficulties" but ultimately what this often boils down to is the realisation of the value of a minority shareholder's holding by the sale of those shares. Given that this realisation of value can otherwise be very difficult in family companies as there is often no market or ability to transfer shares outside the family itself, this outcome can be an extremely valuable one. In other words, unfairly prejudicial actions by majority shareholders can give a minority shareholder an opportunity to cash out of the family business which they would otherwise never have.

Section 994 of the Companies Act 2006

This is a short section but underlying it is some 70 years of case law.

The key provisions of this section are:

> *"Petition by company member*
>
> *(1) A member of a company may apply to the court by petition for an order under this Part on the ground—*
>
> *(a) that the company's affairs are being or have been conducted in a manner that is unfairly prejudicial to the interests of members generally or of some part of its members (including at least himself), or*
>
> *(b) that an actual or proposed act or omission of the company (including an act or omission on its behalf) is or would be so prejudicial.*
>
> ...

> *(2) The provisions of this Part apply to a person who is not a member of a company but to whom shares in the company have been transferred or transmitted by operation of law as they apply to a member of a company.*
>
> …"

Unlike a petition for just and equitable winding up (see below), a petition under s.994 does not require a complainant to come to the court with "clean hands". What this means is that a complainant who has behaved badly is not automatically barred from obtaining a remedy. However, the absence of clean hands is something that the court may have regard to and may, in particular, affect the sort of remedy it is willing to grant. This was a key factor in two of the case studies which appear in Chapter 14.

The way in which s.994 operates to provide a remedy in family business disputes is considered in more detail below.

What is meant by "Unfairly Prejudicial"?

This is not defined in the Companies Act. Nor has it been reduced down to a simple legal definition or list of categories. Judges have regularly confirmed that the categories of unfair prejudice are not closed and that each case must be looked at on its own facts.

However, there are certain well-established principles which provide guidance as to what will or will not amount to unfair prejudice.

The first point to note is that there are two elements to consider, the matter complained of must be both unfair and prejudicial. Section 994 does not provide a mechanism for "no-fault divorce". Without the key element of "unfair prejudice" being present a party's petition to the court will inevitably fail.

The prejudicial part of the equation is normally the easier to prove. Prejudice can be a reduction in the value of a shareholding or other financial damage to the interests of a shareholder, but need not be financial in nature at all. For example, in certain circumstances the removal of a shareholder from an unpaid role as director will be sufficiently prejudicial for the purposes of s.994.

Establishing the unfairness of the actions in question is usually the more complex and difficult part of the exercise. In this respect it does not matter how prejudicial the actions complained are, unless they are also unfair then there will be no remedy.

Four key types or categories of unfairly prejudicial conduct were identified by Warren J, by reference to other leading cases in this area, in the case of *Re. Southern Counties Fresh Foods Ltd [2008] EWHC 2810* as follows:

> *"... a shareholder generally needs to establish one of the following:*
>
> *a. A breach of the terms on which he agreed that the affairs of the company should be conducted;*
>
> *b. That equitable considerations (those referred to by Lord Wilberforce in Ebrahimi v Westbourne Galleries Ltd [1973] AC 360 at 379) arising at the time of the commencement of the relationship or subsequently, make it unfair for those conducting the affairs of the company to rely on their strict legal rights;*
>
> *c. That the board of directors has exceeded the powers vested in them or have exercised their powers for an illegitimate or ulterior purpose; or*
>
> *d. Some event putting an end to the basis on which the parties have entered into association with each other, making it unfair that one shareholder should insist on the continuance of the association.*

Examples of behaviour in family businesses that could fall into one or more of these categories include:

- Failing to comply with the requirements of the Articles of Association, a shareholders' agreement or family charter to the detriment of a minority;

- The removal of a family member as a director of the business when there was a legitimate expectation that significant shareholders would have a place on the board;

- The sale of an asset at an undervalue to the branch of the family holding the majority of the shares;

- The continuance of a family business that has in reality become a lifestyle business for one or more shareholder and which no longer generates any return for the other shareholders.

If the alleged unfairly prejudicial conduct does not fit within one of these categories then this does not mean that a remedy is not available, but it does mean that the merits of the case will need to be given very careful consideration.

More often than not in family businesses the wrong complained of is not a breach of the Articles or the exceeding of directors' powers, but is rather a breach of certain understandings or expectations about how the business should operate. These are addressed by categories (a) and (b) of Warren J's four categories.

It should be noted in relation to category (a) that agreements don't need to be formal to be enforceable. In addition, even where an agreement is not legally binding it may give rise to legitimate expectations which then puts it into category (b).

In relation to category (b) these equitable considerations were first expounded and developed in the case of *Ebrahimi v Westbourne Galleries Ltd [1973] AC 360* (the Ebrahimi case).

In this case it was recognised that there may be informal agreements or understandings between members of a company which in all the circumstances ought to be given effect by the court. Such understandings have been given the shorthand description of "legitimate expectations". By this it is meant expectations on the part of minority shareholders which may make it unfair for the majority to exercise their otherwise legitimate rights in breach of such expectations.

However, caution should be exercised in placing too much weight on this phrase. Judges have been careful to restrict the ambit of this concept. Lord Hoffman in *O'Neill v Phillips [1999] 2 BCLC 1* put it as follows:

> *"The concept of a legitimate expectation should not be allowed to lead a life of its own, capable of giving rise to equitable restraints in circumstances to which the traditional equitable principles have no application."*

In other words, a party may have an expectation, and that expectation may be a legitimate one, but this does not necessarily mean that breaching such an expectation will always be unfairly prejudicial. It is necessary to delve a little deeper into the underlying equitable principles in order to understand why.

The concept of the Quasi-partnership

A key factor as to whether an enforceable "legitimate expectation" arises is whether or not the company in question is, what can be described in shorthand as a "quasi-partnership". Whether or not a company is a quasi-partnership may affect whether any particular step or action is unfairly prejudicial and also has a significant impact on the valuation of a minority shareholding (see chapter 12).

This principle was considered in some detail in the Ebrahami case, which although concerning a petition for winding up expounded some key principles relevant to shareholder disputes generally.

The starting point of the analysis was that a company is more than just a legal construct. As Lord Wilberforce puts it in the Ebrahimi case, explaining the rationale for "just and equitable" relief:

> *"The words are a recognition of the fact that a limited company is more than a mere legal entity with a personality in law of its own: that there is room in company law for recognition of the fact that behind it, or amongst it, there are individual, with rights, expectations and obligations inter se which are not necessarily submerged in the company structure. ... It does, as equity always does, enable the court to subject the exercise of legal rights to equitable considerations;*

> *considerations, that is, of a personal character arising between one individual and another, which may make it unjust, or inequitable, to insist on legal rights, or to exercise them in a particular way."*

In other words the court has the right to step in when legal rights are being exercised in an unfair or oppressive way having regard to wider understandings and expectations as between shareholders.

This will not be the case in all companies, only where there is something over and above the standard commercial relationships which exist in every company. Lord Wilberforce identified three particular elements which may put a company into that category:

> *"The superimposition of equitable considerations requires something more, which typically may include one or probably more of the following elements: (i) an association formed or continued on the basis of a personal relationship, involving mutual confidence this element will often be found where a pre-existing partnership has been converted into a limited company; (ii) an agreement, or understanding that all, or some (for there may be "sleeping" members), of the shareholders shall participate in the conduct of the business; (iii) restriction upon the transfer of the members' interest in the company – so that if confidence is lost, or one member is removed from management, he cannot take out his stake and go elsewhere."*

It can be seen that all three of these elements are likely to be found to a greater or lesser degree in the typical family business.

In particular, family businesses are based on personal relationships and those relationships impart duties of trust and confidence which are absent in purely commercial entities. Likewise, such businesses will often be subject to various informal agreements or understandings which the court is willing to enforce, even when these do not give rise to legally binding rights. Finally, there is often no exit route in place in family businesses, the need for such things as bespoke Articles of Association or shareholders' agreements not being at the forefront of people's minds when all is going well. This can leave a minority shareholder out in the cold and unable to realise any value for their share in the business if they fall out with the majority.

However, it should be noted that not all family businesses will be quasi-partnerships. An example of this is found in the case of *Re. Dinglis Properties Ltd [2019] EWHC 1664 (Ch)*. In this case, brought by a son against his father, it was held that in all the circumstances the family business was not a quasi-partnership. This case is considered in more detail in chapter 14.

The concept of legitimate expectations that will be enforced by the court is not limited to where the company is a full-blown quasi-partnership. An example of the courts enforcing what was in effect a "gentleman's agreement" in a family business (although not in relation to a family member in this instance) can be seen in the judgment in a case brought against the Oyston family, owners of Blackpool FC (*VB Football Assets v Blackpool Football Club (Properties) Limited & Ors [2017] EWHC 2767 (Ch)*).

In this case it was held that a gentleman's agreement existed between the Oyston family and the minority shareholder, Mr Belokon, that notwithstanding his minority shareholding Mr Belokon would be treated as an equal partner. Despite the fact that the agreement did not give rise to specific legal rights it amounted to a legitimate expectation on the part of Mr Belokon.

On the facts of the case it was held that Mr Belokon was not treated as an equal partner, was excluded from management of the company and from participation in profits. The Judge additionally found that the Oyston family had sought to avoid paying out profits via dividends but as a matter of fact payments totalling millions of pounds were disguised dividends to the family.

The actions of the Oyston family were therefore in breach of the legitimate expectations of Mr Belokon and consequently unfairly prejudicial to him pursuant to s.994 of the Companies Act 2006.

As a result of the Judge's findings the Oyston family were required to buy out Mr Belokon for the sum of £31m, which far exceeded the value of the shares on a normal valuation basis, but reflected the disguised dividends.

Remedies – Section 996 of the Companies Act 2006

In terms of remedies the court has a very wide discretion under s.996 of the Companies Act 2006 which states:

> *Powers of the court under this Part*
>
> *(1) If the court is satisfied that a petition under this Part is well founded, it may make such order as it thinks fit for giving relief in respect of the matters complained of.*
>
> *(2) Without prejudice to the generality of subsection (1), the court's order may—*
>
> *(a) regulate the conduct of the company's affairs in the future;*
>
> *(b) require the company—*
>
> *(i) to refrain from doing or continuing an act complained of, or*
>
> *(ii) to do an act that the petitioner has complained it has omitted to do;*
>
> *(c) authorise civil proceedings to be brought in the name and on behalf of the company by such person or persons and on such terms as the court may direct;*
>
> *(d) require the company not to make any, or any specified, alterations in its articles without the leave of the court;*
>
> *(e) provide for the purchase of the shares of any members of the company by other members or by the company itself and, in the case of a purchase by the company itself, the reduction of the company's capital accordingly.*

The breadth of the remedy was described by Mr Justice Patten in the Court of Appeal case *[2005] EWCA Civ 1222 Grace v Biagioli & Ors* as follows, referring to s.461 which was the predecessor of s.996:

> *"Once unfair prejudice is established, the court is given a wide discretion as to the relief which should be granted. Although s.461(1) speaks in terms of relief being granted " in respect of the matters complained of", the court has to look at all the relevant circumstances in deciding what kind of order it is fair to make. It is not limited merely to reversing or putting right the immediate conduct which has justified the making of the order. In Re Bird Precision Bellows [1986]Ch.658, Oliver LJ described the appropriate remedy as one which would "put right and cure for the future the unfair prejudice which the petitioner has suffered at the hands of the other shareholders of the company." The prospective nature of the jurisdiction is reflected in the fact that the court must assess the appropriateness of any particular remedy as at the date of the hearing and not at the date of presentation of the petition; and may even take into account conduct which has occurred between those two dates. The court is entitled to look at the reality and practicalities of the overall situation, past, present and future."*

The purchase of the complainant's shares by the wrongdoer is the most commonly sought and granted remedy. The court can and does grant other remedies in appropriate circumstances but the more bespoke or creative the solution sought the harder it is going to be to get a judgment to this effect. Experience suggests that there is a natural reluctance on the part of Judges to grant relief which is not final, or which might require ongoing monitoring or supervision by the court. The finality of an order exiting the wronged shareholder has a practical attraction in this respect.

Again, Mr Justice Patten in the Grace v Biagioli case expressed this eloquently as follows:

> *"In most cases, the usual order to make will be the one requiring the Respondents to buy out the petitioning shareholder at a price to be fixed by the court. This is normally the most appropriate order to deal with intra company disputes involving small private companies. This is the relief which Mr Grace says that the judge should have granted and which he seeks on this appeal. The reasons for making such an order are in most cases obvious. It will free the petitioner from the company and enable him to extract his share of the value of its business and assets in return for foregoing any future right to dividends.*

> *The company and its business will be preserved for the benefit of the Respondent shareholders, free from his claims and the possibility of future difficulties between shareholders will be removed. In cases of serious prejudice and conflict between shareholders, it is unlikely that any regime or safeguards which the court can impose, will be as effective to preserve the peace and to safeguard the rights of the minority. Although, as Lord Hoffmann emphasised in O'Neill v Phillips, there is no room within this jurisdiction for the equivalent of no-fault divorce, nothing less than a clean break is likely in most cases of proven fault to satisfy the objectives of the court's power to intervene."*

If such an order is made then it is necessary to consider the valuation of the shareholding and this is itself fertile ground for arguments (see chapter 12 and the case studies in chapter 14).

One point to note is that the fact that a party may not be able to afford to buy out the shares at this value will not prevent the court making such an order, although it is a factor the court may take into account. This is something that needs to be understood by anybody on the receiving end of a petition. There is a real risk of bankruptcy if ordered to acquire shares for a sum which cannot be raised.

In such a scenario, where the complaining party is aware that a buyout is not a practical possibility then other routes such as a claim under s.122(1)(g) to wind up the company should potentially be explored.

Finally, s.996 does provide for the possibility of interim remedies, for example an injunction stopping majority shareholders acting in an unfair way. This remedy will only generally be granted where the action being prevented is likely to cause serious harm which cannot be adequately compensated for in damages. The court will look at the balance of convenience, weighing up the harm that could be caused to the applicant as against the impact on the respondents.

An extreme example of such an injunction was seen in the case of *Loveridge v Loveridge [2020] EWCA Civ 1104* which related to a family owned caravan park business. The son, who was the driving force behind the business, withdrew money from the business against the wishes of other shareholders, who then sought to remove him as a director of various companies. The son obtained an urgent injunction preventing his removal and putting him in sole charge of the companies, in support of a s.994 and s.122(1)(g) petition he had issued. This injunction was upheld on the return date, the Judge being swayed by the son's arguments that the importance of his role was such that he should remain at the helm of the companies to protect them.

The other shareholders appealed and were successful. It was held that the son had no legitimate expectations that he should have sole control of the companies and this could not simply be read from the fact that he was the driving force behind the business. In light of this the petitions did not contain an arguable case to justify the continuance of the injunction. The court went further to say that even if there was an arguable case the balance of convenience would not support the continuance of the injunction as damages would be an adequate remedy for any loss caused to the son by the other shareholders in the event of their mismanagement.

CHAPTER SIX

WINDING UP

There are two routes to the winding up of a (solvent) company that are relevant to disputes in family businesses. First, the majority shareholders may seek the winding up of the company under a voluntary liquidation, either a Members Voluntary Liquidation (MVL) or Creditors Voluntary Liquidation (CVL). Secondly, there is a right of shareholders to petition to the court for winding up of the company on just and equitable grounds.

Different considerations apply in relation to insolvent companies which are outside the scope of this book.

Members / Creditors Voluntary Liquidation

A company can be wound up by resolution of its members. A special resolution is required (75% or more of the eligible vote). If the directors are willing to make a statutory declaration of solvency under section 89 of the Insolvency Act 1986 then it will be an MVL, otherwise it will be a CVL.

The members appoint a liquidator to wind up the company and distribute its assets. On the appointment of the liquidator the director's powers cease and the liquidator takes control. Once all creditors are paid, assets realised and distributed the liquidator will deliver a final account, step down and the company will then normally be dissolved.

This process will obviously incur fees and expenses on the part of the liquidator and for this reason a negotiated settlement between shareholders for an orderly winding down of the company and sale of assets is usually preferable. However, if no agreement is possible then it is a route to achieve realisation of assets for shareholders.

In terms of realising value it is best suited to property holding rather than trading companies, but the liquidator can put up a trading business for sale to the highest bidder. This mechanism can therefore be used by majority shareholders to acquire the business of the company via another entity, but is a high-risk strategy if it amounts to unfair prejudice to a minority shareholder (see chapter 9 below).

Just and Equitable Winding Up – Section 122(1)(g) of the Insolvency Act 1996

Under S.122(1)(g) of the Insolvency Act 1986 a shareholder can apply to the court to wind up an otherwise solvent company on "just and equitable" grounds.

The relevant parts of this section are as follows:

> *Circumstances in which company may be wound up by the court.*
>
> *(1) A company may be wound up by the court if—*
>
> ...
>
> *(g) the court is of the opinion that it is just and equitable that the company should be wound up.*

A shareholder is entitled to apply for such a winding up where they have a sufficient interest in the winding up. This means in practice that a fully paid up shareholder must show that there will be monetary surplus after winding up for distribution amongst the company's members. There is also a requirement in most instances that shares have been held for at least 18 months (S.124(2)(b)).

There is no easy definition of what circumstances make it "just and equitable" for a court to wind up a company. Each case is looked at on its own merits. Like s.994, this section is underscored by decades of case law on what circumstances might justify the court stepping in and winding up a company. There is considerable overlap with s.994 in terms of the grounds for seeking relief and what is "unfairly prejudicial" will usually amount to grounds for a "just and equitable" winding up and vice versa. However, this is not always the case (see below).

Examples where winding up on a just and equitable basis has been granted which are of particular relevance to family companies include:

- Failure of the objects or purpose of the company, or the objects have been achieved

- Deadlock

- Fraud or serious misconduct by directors

- Major breaches of Articles or shareholders' agreement

- A serious breach or breakdown of the underlying basis on which a company was set up where there was a relationship of mutual trust and confidence (i.e. a quasi-partnership).

- Exclusion from management in a quasi-partnership

Where it will not be granted

- Lack of confidence in management / disagreements over business direction

- The petition being used to put improper pressure on a company or where there are ulterior motives

- Where there is an alternative remedy and the petitioner is acting unreasonably in not pursuing that remedy

It should be noted that this is an equitable remedy which is in the court's discretion. This means that a person seeking the remedy must come to the court with "clean hands". If they are partially the author of their own misfortune as a result of their own actions then the court is much less likely to assist. Thus, for example, if the person presenting the petition is found to be the essential cause of a breakdown in trust and confidence then the court may decline to grant the remedy sought.

It is also important to note the effect of Section 125(2) of the Insolvency Act 1996 which states:

> *If the petition is presented by members of the company as contributories on the ground that it is just and equitable that the company should be wound up, the court, if it is of opinion—*
>
> *(a) that the petitioners are entitled to relief either by winding up the company or by some other means, and*
>
> *(b) that in the absence of any other remedy it would be just and equitable that the company should be wound up,*
>
> *shall make a winding-up order; but this does not apply if the court is also of the opinion both that some other remedy is available to the petitioners and that they are acting unreasonably in seeking to have the company wound up instead of pursuing that other remedy.*

What this means in practice is that even if a case for winding up on equitable grounds is clearly established the court may refuse to grant the relief on the basis that there is an alternative remedy and it is unreasonable for the complainant not to pursue that remedy (s.125(2)). A court is unlikely to relish winding up an otherwise healthy company and will therefore look closely at such alternatives before granting an order for winding up.

Alternative remedies can include an offer by the respondents to buy the complainant's shares at a fair value or the fact that the complainant might have a more appropriate remedy under s.994.

An example of these considerations being applied in practice can be found in the case of *Re Brand & Harding Ltd [2014] EWHC 247 (Ch).*

This was a family business that was in effect a large farm. The petitioner was two sisters, the respondent a third elder sister. All three had been appointed directors of the family business on their father's death.

The two younger sisters fell out with the older one resulting in acrimony and accusations and counter-accusations. Eventually the two younger sisters petitioned for just and equitable winding up on the basis that the business could not be run properly in light of the disagreements between them. The elder sister opposed this on the basis that she should be entitled to run it alone for the benefit of all.

The court looked at five questions that had originally been proposed in the Ebrahami case (see chapter 5) as a test of the elements required in the court's consideration of a request to wind up on just and equitable grounds:

1. Was the company intended to be run as a quasi-partnership?

2. Was it in fact run as a quasi-partnership?

3. Was there a reason for the court to intervene?

4. Whether there was an alternative remedy, other than winding up, that the petitioners were unreasonably failing to pursue?

5. Whether in all the circumstances it was just and equitable for the court to exercise its discretion to wind the company up

It was held in this case that all five tests from the Ebrahimi case were satisfied. It was the intention of the father, shared at the time by the mother and sisters that they would run the farm together. It was run like a partnership, all the sisters taking part. The disputes between the sisters justified the court intervening and there was no alternative remedy as it was clear that the elder sister was not going to sell her shares to her siblings and she could not afford to buy out the others. Accordingly it was just & equitable to wind up.

It is important to note that the fact that mutual trust and confidence has broken down in a quasi-partnership company will not, on its own, justify winding up on just and equitable grounds. This was the finding in the case of *Badyal v Badyal & Ors [2019] EWCA Civ 1644*. Here, three brothers originally traded together in a partnership and subsequently also in a company. Relationships broke down and one brother brought a s.994 petition and subsequently a s.122(1)(g) petition against his brothers in relation to the company. Both failed at trial, largely as a result of findings about the petitioning brother's own behaviour.

He appealed on one point, which was that the Judge was wrong in finding that a mutual breakdown in trust and confidence, which all parties had accepted had occurred, was not sufficient in itself to justify winding up on just and equitable grounds.

The Court of Appeal firmly supported the Judge's ruling on the basis that the breakdown in confidence was due to the petitioner's own behaviour. Unlike in a true partnership case where the fact of a breakdown in trust and confidence was sufficient to justify dissolution, the grounds for just and equitable winding up were not made out. It was to an extent an affirmation of the principle seen in s.994 cases, which is that there is no "no fault divorce". Despite this, the door was clearly left open by the court for just and equitable winding up to be granted where the breakdown in trust and confidence was severe, preventing the company from functioning properly and was not the fault of the petitioner. In such circumstances a petition may well be successful.

Overlap with s.994 of the Companies Act 2006

The rights provided by s.122(1)(g) and s.994 are separate and distinct but the relationship between the two has been complicated in the past and there is historic case law to the effect that "unfair prejudice" and what is "just & equitable" amount to one and the same thing.

However following the Court of Appeal case of *Re Neath Rugby Limited [2009] EWCA Civ 291* it appears to be clearly established that they operate in parallel and whilst the circumstances which amount to unfair prejudice and grounds to wind up on just & equitable grounds are often the same, this is not always the case. In particular, something that it is not unfairly prejudicial may nevertheless justify winding up on just and equitable grounds.

This principle was affirmed in the case of *Amin v Amin [2009] EWHC 3356 (Ch)* in which the Judge indicated that whilst he had not been willing to grant relief for unfair prejudice he would have been willing to countenance winding up on a just & equitable basis. He was unable to do so in this case as there was no claim in the petition for relief on this basis.

This does not mean that in most cases it would be appropriate to petition for relief under s.994 and/or relief under s.122(1)(g). This has been judicially discouraged in the past, and Practice Direction 49B – Order under section 127 of the Insolvency Act 1986 states as follows:

> *"Attention is drawn to the undesirability of asking as a matter of course for a winding up order as an alternative to an order under section 994 of the Companies Act 2006. The petition should not ask for a winding up order unless that is the remedy which the petitioner prefers or it is thought that it may be the only remedy to which the petitioner is entitled."*

This principle has also been affirmed in case law. In light of this the better course is usually to nail your colours to the mast from the outset and choose whether to proceed under s.994 or s.122(1)(g). The key points to consider in terms of choosing the s.122(1)(g) route being (a) whether in all the circumstances winding up would be a better remedy and (b) where there is obvious prejudice but the unfairness is less clear cut.

CHAPTER SEVEN

OTHER CAUSES OF ACTION UNDER THE COMPANIES ACT 2006

Derivative claims

As noted in chapter 3, whilst shareholders have some personal remedies in relation to breaches of the Articles of Association, the company itself is generally the proper complainant when, for example, directors are behaving badly / breaching their fiduciary duties. However, what happens when those directors control the board and therefore block the company from taking any action?

Shareholders have long been able to bring a claim in the name of a company against those guilty of wrongdoing, but this right was very restricted. In essence it was only possible where the wrongdoing amounted to an "equitable fraud" against the company and the wrongdoers were in control of the company.

The claim is brought by the shareholder in the name of and on behalf of the company and is called a derivative claim because the shareholders' right to claim derives from the company's right to claim. The most important point to note is that the proceeds of any claim belong to the company and not the shareholder.

A statutory derivative claim was introduced by ss. 260 – 263 of the Companies Act 2006. These sections provide a mechanism for a claim to be brought in respect of a cause of action arising from an actual or proposed act or omission involving negligence, default, breach of duty or breach of trust by a director of the company.

This has made the remedy less restrictive in scope but has introduced a two-stage process, the first stage of which is to obtain the permission of the court. The court will look at the claim through the eyes of the company in deciding whether to grant permission. In particular it will consider whether a director of the company acting in accordance with their duties under the Companies Act would seek to continue the claim. If the court concludes that no director would do so then permission will not be granted.

This is no mere formality. The burden of proof is on the person seeking to bring the claim to establish a prima facie case to bring the action, that the claims are sustainable and the sums at stake worthwhile.

The proceedings are inevitably expensive given the need for extensive advocacy in this respect and although an indemnity for the costs from the company can be sought (Civil Procedure Rules 19.9E), it is not guaranteed to be ordered.

In the context of family businesses this route might be appropriate where, for example, a significant minority shareholder wishes to retain their shares and where there is a specific act of wrongdoing by controlling directors who also control the majority of the shares, leading to a quantified loss on the part of the company which the directors decline to pursue.

An example of a case where permission to pursue a derivative action was given and the interaction with s.994 considered is that of *Re Eldington Holdings Ltd [2010] EWHC 1539 (Ch)*. The Judge deals with the assertion that permission should not be granted because s.994 was an alternative route as follows:

> "*In the present action, the Applicant is not seeking to be bought out. He commenced these proceedings, with the support of 35 other minority shareholders, seeking financial remedies for misconduct against the two directors personally, and now an order for restitution from Eldington. Such orders could not be made on an unfair prejudice petition, albeit that the court could by way of remedy authorise the bringing of proceedings in the name of the company by the petitioner: section 996(2)(c) . But that would then give rise to a subsequent and further set of proceedings. I consider that given what is at the heart of the present case, a derivative action is entirely appropriate and therefore the theoretical availability to the Applicant of proceedings by way of an unfair prejudice petition is not a reason to refuse permission.*"

This quote gives a steer as to the kind of cases where a derivative action would be appropriate. In practice this remedy is unlikely to be the most attractive route to resolve most disputes within family businesses and minority shareholders will probably look instead at the other statutory remedies that are available.

Rectification of the register

The court has the power to rectify the register of members (shareholders) under s.125 of the Companies Act 2006 which provides as follows:

> *(1)* *If—*
>
> *(a)* *the name of any person is, without sufficient cause, entered in or omitted from a company's register of members, or*
>
> *(b)* *default is made or unnecessary delay takes place in entering on the register the fact of any person having ceased to be a member, the person aggrieved, or any member of the company, or the company, may apply to the court for rectification of the register.*
>
> *(2)* *The court may either refuse the application or may order rectification of the register and payment by the company of any damages sustained by any party aggrieved.*
>
> *(3)* *On such an application the court may decide any question relating to the title of a person who is a party to the application to have his name entered in or omitted from the register, whether the question arises between members or alleged members, or between members or alleged members on the one hand and the company on the other hand, and generally may decide any question necessary or expedient to be decided for rectification of the register.*

As it is necessary to be a member to petition under s.994, it can sometimes be the case that a valid transfer of shares or transmission of shares on death is declined to be registered by those in control of the board and/or the company's books and records. In such circumstances this section can be used as a route to get an initial court ruling on membership of the company (see Chapter 11 for more on this).

CHAPTER EIGHT

ALTERNATIVE DISPUTE RESOLUTION (ADR) AND OFFERS OF SETTLEMENT

Pursuing a petition under either s.994 or s.122(1)(g) can be prohibitively expensive with an uncertain outcome. For those reasons it is always worth exploring alternative dispute resolution (ADR). This comes in many forms:

- Negotiation in correspondence / offers of settlement
- Round table meetings
- Structured negotiation (e.g. mediation)
- Expert determination / opinion

The aim of such discussions is to arrive at negotiated settlement and this is usually progressed by making offers of settlement.

Offers of settlement

These are normally made in correspondence and are "without prejudice" meaning that they cannot be shown to the Judge or referred to in court except in limited circumstances.

They can take different forms:

- "Calderbank" – typically an all-inclusive offer made in writing to resolve the dispute on specified terms.
- Part 36 – an offer made pursuant to Part 36 of the Civil Procedure Rules which is "plus costs" and has certain specified effects in terms of legal costs if the recipient does worse at trial than the offer.

- O'Neill offer – a particular kind of offer made in shareholder disputes (see below).

In a family business dispute a typical offer might be one on the part of the majority shareholders to buy out the shares of the minority for a specified sum of money. This may prompt a counter-offer on the part of the minority shareholders seeking a larger sum of money. It should be noted in this context that a counter-offer is treated as the formal rejection of the original offer. This means that it is no longer possible for the person making the counter-offer to go back and say they accept the original offer, which technically is no longer open for acceptance (unless the maker of the original is willing to repeat it or is willing to treat the acceptance as a counter-offer which they in turn accept).

All such offers must be carefully considered by the recipient as they can have a significant impact with regard to the recovery of legal costs. Put simply, a party who goes to trial and fails to do better than such an offer may find that they have to pay a greater proportion of the other side's legal costs or even have to pay such costs from the date the offer was made despite otherwise being the winner in the action. This is particularly the case if the offer is compliant with Part 36, in which case there are prescribed benefits for the person making the offer including in relation to the calculation of the costs which are payable and interest on those costs.

It can be seen that an understanding of the value of the business, and hence of individual shareholdings, is critical to evaluating such offers. This also something that court must grapple with if it is asked to assess whether an offer is a reasonable one.

An additional factor in shareholder disputes is that a properly constructed offer on the part of a respondent to an unfair prejudice claim can also have the effect of negating any unfair prejudice such that any petition risks being struck out (see the discussion about O'Neill offers below).

If it is not possible to agree a value for the shares but there is effectively an agreement that one party should buy out the other then an expert valuer can be employed to resolve the dispute. The parties can appoint their own valuers or opt to jointly appoint a valuer to give an opinion on the value of the shares based on an agreed set of facts. In the latter case the parties can either agree that the valuation is just a starting point for wider discussions or they can agree to be bound by the valuation.

This is also the effect of what has become known as an "O'Neill offer". This offer is named after a formulation advanced by the Judge in the case of *O'Neill v Phillips [1999] UKHL 24*. A correctly drafted O'Neill offer can be very powerful. It can cause a petition to be struck out at an early stage if the receiving party refuses it and the court is of the view that there is no basis on which they would do better than trial or no other reason why it would be unfair to force them to accept the offer.

Standard Form of "O'Neill offer"

The standard form of offer is as follows:

> [We will / We invite you to agree that you will] purchase [name's] shares at a valuation to be conducted by an independent accountant to be appointed in default of agreement by the President of the Institute of Chartered Accountants in England and Wales.
>
> The valuation will be on the following basis:
>
> a. [Name's] shareholding will be valued at a fair value as between a willing buyer and a willing seller on a pro rata basis [with no discount for minority holding] , and on the basis that the Company is a going concern ;
>
> b. The valuer shall take account of the assets, profitability and prospects of the Company;
>
> c. The valuation will be as at the date of this letter ;
>
> d. The valuation will proceed on the basis that [e.g. any increase in [Name's] remuneration since [Name's] removal from the Company is notionally added back, as will the value of any assets transferred out of the Company at an undervalue;

e. For the purposes of making submissions to the valuer, each party will have full access to all financial information concerning the Company;

f. The valuer will act as expert not arbitrator, and shall not give reasons for his decision;

g. The valuer will have power to determine who shall bear the costs of the valuation.

If making such an offer a majority shareholder should consider making the offer "plus costs" thus giving greater costs protection and, if proceedings are on foot, significantly increasing the reasonableness of the offer. In the O'Neill case itself the failure to offer payment of legal costs when the offer was made some way into the litigation process was found to be a justified reason for the respondent to decline to accept it.

Where a minority shareholder is making a reverse offer then they should consider adding a time period within which the acquisition must be made after the valuation to give greater certainty in this respect.

A case study on how the court approaches offers

In the Court of Appeal judgment in the case of *Re. Sprintroom [2019] EWCA Civ 932 (Ch)* the appeal Judges looked closely at a number of different offers of settlement that had been made by the respondent to the petition against the background of claims by the respondent that these were fair and reasonable to such a degree that they negated the unfair prejudice and therefore the petition should fail. The conclusion was that when looked at in their context none of the offers remedied the unfair prejudice which it had been found had been suffered by the petitioner. The judgment highlights some key points and considerations in this respect which can be summarised as follows:

- An O'Neill offer should not be considered a "trump card" that will inevitably result in the petition being struck out if not accepted;

- It must be considered in all the circumstances and what must be shown is that the continued pursuit of the petition in light of the offer would effectively be an abuse of process or mean that the petition was bound to fail;

- What has to be considered is the terms of the offer, the circumstances in which it was made and the reasons why it was rejected;

- An offer of fixed sum can be fair if it is justified by objective facts or the product of an agreed process of valuation;

- The ability of the recipient to properly evaluate the offer at the time it is made is an important factor;

- The offer must take into account allegations of, for example, diversions of assets which have devalued the company. If these are made on reasonable grounds then even if they are ultimately not upheld it is reasonable for a recipient of an offer to reject it if they are not taken into account;

- The offer must be capable of being performed, i.e. the offeror must be able to demonstrate the means to be able to afford it;

- The timing of the offer is important, for example it may be given less importance if made at some point prior to a breakdown in relations or in a different context.

In this case the Judge at first instance had held that he was unable to determine the reasonableness of the offers and therefore their impact on the petition generally without an assessment of the value of the shares. This approach was rejected by the Court of Appeal which concluded that, by reference to various of the factors identified above, there was sufficient material to establish that the rejection of the offers did not fatally undermine the petition.

The Court of Appeal also stressed that in any event the effect of a reasonable offer is not binary in the sense that it must lead to the petition being dismissed or must be disregarded completely. They put it as follows:

> *"Once the court has considered the reasonableness of an offer, it may take one of four courses. If the offer made was entirely reasonable and the petitioner acted unreasonably in rejecting it, it is open to the court to conclude that the unfair prejudice petition fails. The court should bear in mind the potentially draconian effect of that conclusion if the petitioner is then forced indefinitely to remain a minority shareholder in a business in the management of which he is no longer involved. Secondly, it is open to a court to conclude that the unfair prejudice petition succeeds but that the appropriate remedy is an order directing the buy out of the shares at the price that was offered, perhaps subject to adjustments to take account of the passage of time and changes in the market or to redress the impact of the unfairly prejudicial conduct on the value of the company. This course would have the advantage of avoiding the delay and expense of a subsequent hearing and the instruction of experts to value the shares. Thirdly a court may conclude that the fair response is to treat the offer as a factor relevant to the award of costs following the conclusion of the proceedings. It may be appropriate in some cases to modify an order that costs follow the event so as to recognise the making and rejection of the offer. This is an approach recognised by Lord Hoffmann in O'Neill v Phillips: see p. 1106E – H. Fourthly, of course, the court could conclude that the making of the offer has no effect on the success of the petition, the appropriate method for valuing the shares for the buy out order or the petitioner's entitlement to his costs of the proceedings."*

The important point to take away is that an offer to buy a minority shareholder out of the business, particularly if made in the O'Neill format, can be a powerful tool, having an effect beyond just the question of liability for legal costs at the conclusion of the matter.

Mediation

Mediation is a process in which a neutral third party leads a structured negotiation with the aim of assisting parties in a dispute to achieve a negotiated settlement. The neutral third party is called a mediator. Mediation is an effective way of resolving shareholder disputes in family businesses faster and at considerably less cost than pursuing court proceedings.

Parties to such disputes are often concerned about saying anything which can be "used against them". This can constrain settlement discussions. Mediation is conducted on a strictly 'without prejudice' basis. This means that the matters discussed in the mediation, or documents produced, cannot be shown to the court or otherwise employed in any litigation between the parties.

Unlike in litigation, the parties and their advisers remain in complete control and ultimately decide whether and how a case will be settled. Any party to mediation can bring the mediation to a halt at any point, should they choose to do so. This means that a party who is properly represented with a competent mediator on board is not going to be forced or bullied into a deal or settlement against their wishes. This idea of being "bullied" is a recurring theme in disputes between siblings and mediation is a good forum to ventilate these issues and hopefully get past them.

An unreasonable failure to consider or pursue mediation (or other forms of alternative dispute resolution) can result in the court imposing costs penalties on the party in default. This could mean, for example, that a "winning" party is denied an award of their legal costs in whole or in part on the basis that if they had agreed to mediate then the matter could have been resolved more cost-effectively.

The role of the mediator

The job of the mediator is to listen to the parties and try to identify common ground that may form the basis of a settlement and help the parties to reach that settlement. Rather than being judgmental, the approach of the mediator will be to endeavour to facilitate constructive and productive negotiations. The mediator will not ultimately make a decision on any issue.

Traditional mediators take a purely facilitative approach and will not offer an opinion on any issue. However, many mediators prefer a more evaluative approach and they may express their personal opinions on issues. This can sometimes be helpful as it can be useful to have a third party's view on the merits of an issue. This is particularly the case in family business disputes where both sides can sometimes value the input of an experienced neutral party.

Approaching mediation in the context of a family business dispute

The aim of mediation is to achieve a negotiated settlement of the dispute. Accordingly, the parties and their lawyers should try not to see themselves purely as advocates of their cause. The key to a successful mediation is flexibility in considering the position of the other parties by reference to a risk analysis of a party's own position.

This means actively listening to what the other side is saying, something which does not always happen when relationships have broken down. Listening can reveal what lies at the heart of any dispute, which like in any personal relationship, may not be what the parties are currently arguing about.

Lawyers should set aside their combative instincts and try and view the situation from a more neutral position, from that of an outside observer. They should get away from the "point scoring" approach typical of much pre-action correspondence and instead think about how a dialogue can be started. This may not be easy in family business disputes when emotions are high and bridges appear to have broken, but a good mediator can help the process along.

The role of the mediator, and the lawyers instructed by the parties, should be to help steer the parties in their decision making. This is where a commercial litigator should be firmly placing the emphasis on "commercial" rather than "litigator".

A negotiated settlement is invariably a compromise. It depends upon the parties putting forward terms of settlement that realistically balance what they believe they might achieve in litigation against the risks of losing.

Whether a settlement is ultimately reached will depend upon whether the terms that are offered are considered to be a satisfactory outcome having regard to the risk analysis that has been carried out by each party. If the terms on offer are not as good as the risk analysis suggests would be appropriate then either a commercial decision can be made to accept them in any event or it can be accepted that the mediation has failed. In this respect it can be necessary to be creative, to find something else that can be added to the pot, which may only of nominal or symbolic value, but which in the context of family relationships is meaningful. This can make all the difference in getting a settlement across the line.

A classic definition of a successful settlement is that both parties go away slightly dissatisfied. This indicates that both sides have compromised to reach an agreement they can live with. This might sound to some lawyers like an odd thing to be striving to achieve on behalf of their client, but set against the costs and risks of litigation it is an appropriate objective.

Practical issues in relation to share acquisitions

One of the key issues that needs to be addressed is the affordability of any settlement. For example, can the majority family shareholders afford to buy out the minority shareholder at a fair value?

One of the advantages of settlement discussions / mediation is that a settlement can be structured to make it affordable. This can include payment being made over a period of time or the acquisition of shares being made in tranches. It can also provide for protection for the acquiring party in the event that the minority shareholder has been guilty of some financial misconduct which is not currently known about. Whilst the court has a wide remit in terms of remedies in a s.994 petition it is unlikely to be creative in this respect except if there is broad agreement between the parties on the terms of such a deal. A Judge will be particularly reluctant to order anything which lacks finality in terms of resolving the matter or which may require future monitoring or input from the court.

Another matter which can be addressed is tax efficiency. There may be advantages to the majority shareholders in dealing with the purchase via a share buyback by the company (if, for example, it has sufficient distributable profits). The minority shareholder may be concerned about the impact of the structure of any deal on their ability to claim tax relief. It is therefore sensible to obtain tax advice at an early stage in discussions to avoid the scenario of agreeing the structure for settlement but discovering adverse tax consequences or a more tax-efficient route with the consequent need to re-open the discussions.

In terms of documenting any settlement, in the simplest of cases this can take the form of the acceptance of an offer creating a binding agreement for purchase of shares which is then effected by the execution of a stock transfer form. If proceedings are in progress then this will also need to recorded in a consent order.

In more complex cases, it is usual for a detailed settlement agreement to be prepared which is also effectively a share purchase agreement and includes warranties and covenants. Warranties may be required where, for example, the departing party has had a continuing role in the company but there has been a lack of transparency and hence the purchasing party wants to protect their position against unknowns. The warranties might include the confirmation by the selling shareholder that there has been no financial misconduct on their part or no transactions other than at arms-length and on normal commercial terms. Covenants can be reasonably be expected where a minority shareholder is cashing out of the company at an undiscounted value. In such circumstances a covenant that they will not compete with the company for a reasonable period are not unreasonable and often imposed in the normal commercial sphere.

Expert determination

As noted above, one potential settlement outcome is that the parties agree to jointly appoint an expert valuer to arrive at a binding decision with regard to the valuation of the shares. This can be accompanied by an agreement that one party will buy out the other at the value determined by the expert. This is in effect the outcome if an O'Neill offer is accepted but sometimes more bespoke agreements to this effect are negotiated.

The key things to consider in relation to any agreement to submit a matter to expert determination are as follows:

- How is the identity of the expert going to be agreed?
- If no agreement is reached how are they going to be appointed? In this respect there are bodies such as the Institute of Chartered Accountants for England and Wales who have an appointment scheme on the application of the parties.
- How is the expert going to be paid? It is normal to split the cost equally between the parties but sometimes the expert is given the

power to direct that their costs should be paid by one party rather than the other (e.g. if one party has behaved unreasonably).

- What powers is the expert going to have in terms of determining in the structure of the process? If an appointment scheme is used then there may be established rules or the expert may have their own process which they wish to use. Otherwise the parties need to define the process.

What needs to be addressed in the process is:

- Equality of arms in terms of access to information (particularly if one party has been excluded from the company).

- Transparency – i.e. communications with the expert should normally be copied to the other party.

- Form of submissions – what is the format of the submissions to be made by the parties setting out their case in relation to valuation (e.g. written statements with key documents appended, or should there be separate process for exchanging documentary evidence).

- Sequence of submissions – are they to be made simultaneously or sequentially? Do the parties then have a right of reply? When are submissions considered closed?

- Timescale – ideally a fixed timescale should be imposed on the exercise but in practice the expert may resist this the time taken may be outside of his control if the parties don't fully cooperate or engage in battles about the supply of documentation or information.

- Approach to valuation – whether a specified valuation method should be used or whether this is left to the expert to decide?

- Format of the expert's decision – often this is stated to be "without reasons", in other words a simple figure for value without an analysis of how this is arrived at. The reasons for this are finality (to avoid a disappointed party from picking over the analysis with a view to picking holes in it) and cost.

Expert determination can be a good route to achieving a certain outcome if the only real dispute is over valuation, but it can be a high-risk strategy. There are very limited grounds to appeal an expert determination. For this reason proper consideration needs to be given to the appropriate format and process to achieve a fair and objective valuation based on all the relevant facts. In larger cases each party will often have their own expert accountant on board to assist with determining the process and to help prepare submissions and analyse the submissions made by the other party with a view to pointing the expert in the right direction for their client.

CHAPTER NINE

ADVISING MAJORITY SHAREHOLDERS

Like divorces, shareholder disputes often involve two sides with unequal firepower. One side holds and controls the assets and access to information, whilst the other is looking in from the outside and may have limited funds to fight a case with. This means that very different concerns arise depending upon which side you are on.

The majority shareholders hold most of the cards in shareholder disputes. They can often use the concept of majority rule and their powers under statute and the Articles of Association to exclude a minority shareholder from a role in the company, turn off the tap in terms of that shareholder's income from the company and deny them all but the most basic financial and other information.

Such actions may or may not then amount to unfair prejudice, but the burden of proof is on the minority shareholder and the onus on them to take action to obtain a remedy.

However, majority shareholders must be careful not to dig themselves into a hole. It should not be forgotten that as a respondent to a petition a majority shareholder is potentially personally liable to (a) acquire the shares of the minority shareholder at a fair value and (b) pay the legal costs associated with the action (their own costs and a large percentage of their opponents). This significant potential personal liability means that majority shareholders should mitigate the risk if they can.

In relation to "fair value" the key fact which majority shareholders need to be aware of is that this fair value may not be calculated on the normal commercial basis which would assume a discount for a minority shareholding. If the petitioner was successful and it was found to be a quasi-partnership company then the majority shareholders may have to buy out the minority at a pro rata value (see chapter 12).

One of the main tasks for those advising majority shareholders can be to rein them in. The emotional nature of such disputes within family businesses means that a breakdown in relations can cause parties to go nuclear when actually something a little less drastic would achieve the objective. For example, a minority shareholder creating difficulties / conflict at board level as a director may be capable of being removed from office by majority shareholders. That may be sufficient to remove the actual problem but what often happens is that they are also removed as an employee, their remuneration stopped and access to information restricted. Removal as a director in the case of bad behaviour can more easily be objectively justified and is therefore unlikely to be held as being unfair. Going further than this may be much harder to justify and give the minority shareholder an unfair prejudice claim.

Majority shareholders may also be tempted to turn off the tap of money to minority shareholders by not declaring dividends and/or increasing their own remuneration as directors to soak up profits instead. This is what happened in the case of *CF Booth Ltd [2017] EWHC 457 (Ch).*

The company in question was a family owned recycling business. The directors were the majority shareholders. Over a long period the company stopped paying any dividends, the directors' salaries increased to well above any reasonable market rates and the directors used company money to purchase a fleet of luxury cars and a yacht to which they, but not the minority shareholders, had access to. The minority shareholders did receive offers to buy them out but these offers were well below any realistic market valuation of their shares.

The minority family members petitioned the court under s.994. They claimed that the actions of the majority family members were unfair due to their excessive remuneration and failure to pay dividends. The court found that the minority family members had been unfairly prejudiced as the directors had breached their duties under the Companies Act 2006 in relation to both their remuneration and the policy not to pay dividends.

These duties, as summarised by the Judge, were:

- To exercise the power to recommend or not recommend a dividend for the purposes for which the power was conferred (section 171(b) of the Companies Act 2006)

- To reach the conclusion (dividend or no dividend) that they consider, in good faith, would be most likely to promote the success of the company for the benefit of its members as a whole (section 172 of the Companies Act 2006)

- To exercise independent judgment (section 173 of the Companies Act 2006)

The Judge held that what the majority family members did was primarily in their personal interests and not the interests of the company. As a result, they were ordered to buy out the minority family members at a fair value.

Another trap which majority shareholders can fall into is to use company money to fight a minority shareholder. The position in this respect was put quite clearly by the Judge (Hoffman J) in the case of *Re Crossmore Electrical and Civil Engineering Ltd (1989) 5 BCC 37* (a case under s.459) as follows:

> "*The company is a nominal party to the sec. 459 petition, but in substance the dispute is between the two shareholders. It is a general principle of company law that the company's money should not be expended on disputes between the shareholders; see Pickering v. Stephenson (1872) L.R. 14 Eq. 322. Consequently it seems to me clear that such expenditure on defending the sec. 459 petition would not be in the ordinary course of business ...*"

Numerous cases since then have endorsed this dim view on the part of the courts on company money being used in what is essentially a dispute between members.

It is not always the case that expenditure on legal costs by the company in relation to such a dispute will be wrongful. Permission can be sought from the court in exceptional cases. In addition, the company will be a respondent to any petition and is entitled to legal representation and advice on its own position. However, if that advice spills over into tactical or strategic advice for the benefit of the majority shareholders it will have crossed the line.

It is also possible that sight of the advice may be sought by the minority shareholders and it may be difficult to assert privilege on behalf of the company against such disclosure. This was the finding of Harman J in the case of *Re Hydrosan Ltd [1991] BCC 19* which cited with approval the Crossmore case referred to above. The minority shareholders sought copies of solicitors' bills delivered to the company, who resisted on the grounds of privilege. It was found that the nature of the petition being a dispute between shareholders meant that the company could not assert privilege in this context.

On a practical note, there is no fundamental problem with one law firm / lawyer acting for both the company and the majority shareholders in a dispute (subject to any specific conflict of interests) but care should be taken to ring fence the matters with, for example, separate files being opened for each and clear distinctions made between work done for the company and which may be charged to the company, and work done for shareholders. This will enable legal privilege to be more easily preserved and the rebuttal of suggestions that company money is being wrongly deployed.

In relation to what is permissible expenditure, given that much of the documentation relating to a shareholder dispute may be held by the company it will need to take a pro-active role in the disclosure process in any action and is therefore entitled to use lawyers in that context. It can also seek advice and representation in relation to any order or judgment which might affect the company. Otherwise, the general rule is that the company should stay out of the dispute.

In the Hydrosan case the Judge made it clear that in particularly egregious cases of the use of company money by majority shareholders then this can give rise to a separate claim of unfair prejudice:

> "*In the present case, if the company's funds were employed in financing the defence to the first sec. 459 petition that, it is said, must be a*

> *wrongful misapplication of funds and would warrant the present second sec. 459 petition."*

In summary, misuse of company money will bolster an unfair prejudice claim or even create one where there might otherwise not have been one.

It should be noted that the bar on use of company money does not apply to actions brought genuinely for the benefit of the company. Thus for example, if a family business has removed a shareholder as a director because of alleged misappropriation of money or assets then the company can seek legal advice on any claim against that director and expend money on pursuing a viable claim. This is a classic example of attack being the best form of defence, the excluded shareholder then being on the back foot and having to personally fund the defence of a claim brought by the company. This may encourage them to the negotiating table more quickly than otherwise.

The key question is whether it is a bona fide claim that would be pursued regardless of any shareholder dispute. If it is found to be essentially a tactic to apply pressure on the minority shareholder then it carries the risk of strengthening the claim for unfair prejudice. However, if there is a genuine claim for loss or damage on the part of the company against a minority shareholder then this can be properly deployed by the shareholders in control of the company.

There are various other tactics which may be used by majority shareholders to improve their own position or weaken that of the minority shareholder. These can include:

- amending the Articles of Association
- dilution of shares
- company re-organisations
- liquidation (insolvent / solvent)

These are particularly relevant where the majority shareholders hold 75% or more of the shares entitled to vote, thus enabling them to pass a special resolution. With this power they can, for example, amend the Articles to add a provision entitling them to purchase the shares of a minority shareholder or even introduce "good leaver / bad leaver" provisions in relation to the compulsory purchase of shares of a departing director.

The right to amendment of the Articles is not without limitations. Such amendment cannot have the effect of removing rights or entitlements that have already accrued under the previous Articles. Furthermore, the changes must be bona fide in the interests of the company as whole. An amendment which cannot be commercially justified or which is obviously in bad faith can give rise to a personal action on the part of an affected shareholder.

An example of this in practice can be found in the case of *Re. Charterhouse Capital Ltd [2014] EWHC 1410 (Ch)* where the actions of the majority shareholders in relation to the amendment of Articles of Association to add "drag along" provisions to acquire a minority shareholder's holding were the subject of a s.994 petition. Here it was held that the amendments were done for the benefit of the company as a whole and the petitioner failed to establish any special understanding or agreements in relation to his personal position that made it unfair.

The general point to note in this respect is that all such actions on the part of majority shareholders will need to be capable of being objectively justified if they are to avoid giving rise to a claim of unfair prejudice. Simple application of a "sniff test" is recommended. If it feels wrong or unfair then the minority shareholder will probably have the starting point for a claim.

One tactic which may be employed is to place a company into a members voluntary liquidation (MVL). This may be a good option where for example the company is non-trading or just holds easily liquidated assets. The minority shareholder can normally have no complaint if they are treated like all other shareholders and receive the fair pro rata value of their shares.

However, often an MVL is used with the aim of the majority shareholders then acquiring the assets of the company at a low value. The fact that the company has gone into liquidation does not mean that a minority shareholder no longer has a remedy. If the sole or main purpose of an MVL appears to be to enable the assets of the company to be acquired by a connected party at a low value then a minority shareholder will have a potential claim for unfair prejudice. They can then seek that their shares are purchased on the basis of the value prior to the liquidation.

Even if the company has been dissolved following the conclusion of a liquidation there is scope for the company to be restored to the register in order for disaffected minority shareholders to appoint new liquidators and investigate the circumstances of the MVL, see *Re. Core VCT plc (in liquidation) [2019] EWHC 540 (Ch).*

CHAPTER TEN

ADVISING MINORITY SHAREHOLDERS

The grounds for bringing a s.994 or s.122(1)(g) petition or a derivative claim are set out elsewhere in this book. Some of the key considerations when advising minority shareholders can be summarised here as follows:

- What is the nature of the company – is it a quasi-partnership?
- What is the value of the company?
- Are the actions complained of breaches of formal rights or informal understandings?
- In the latter case, do those understandings amount to "legitimate expectations?
- Are the actions complained of "unfair" having regard to all the circumstances?
- Have they caused prejudice?
- What evidence is available?
- What is the most appropriate legal remedy?
- Is ADR appropriate and if so when?

Otherwise, advising minority shareholders at a strategic level is to some extent the mirror image of advising majority shareholders, but there are subtle points of difference as well as some unique issues to consider.

As discussed in chapter 3, the formal rights of shareholders are relatively limited. Once on the outside of a company they have few rights to information or visibility of the day to day functioning of the company. There are however a few practical pressure points that can be employed to get the majority shareholders' attention and perhaps get to them to the negotiating table at an early stage. The main ones are:

- Calling a general meeting;
- A request for audited accounts;
- Making reasonable requests for information;
- Monitoring use of company money (see chapter 9);
- Involving the bank;
- Bringing employment related proceedings.

With 10% of the voting shares you can call a shareholders meeting with the aim of ventilating the issues. This might be the catalyst for negotiations or the meeting could be tightly controlled and shut down by the majority shareholders with little achieved.

Also with 10% a shareholder can require that the company's accounts are audited, but as noted in chapter 3 this is not as exciting as it sounds. It merely requires the company to appoint auditors who then certify the filed accounts accordingly. The minority shareholder has no rights to any input into the choice of auditor and nor can they direct the auditor to make investigations. Note also that this is a longer-term strategy as you must request the audit at least one month before the end of the financial year and the accounts for that financial year (which may not be produced for many months) will then have to be audited. There is no right to seek the auditing of historic accounts.

There is also some merit in making reasonable requests for information about the company, particularly if this information has been provided previously before any dispute. The unreasonable failure to supply information, even where there is no legal obligation on the part of the majority shareholders / directors to do so, is potentially unfair. The key point to note is that they should be reasonable. Bombarding the directors with unrealistic scattergun requests may have the opposite effect, supporting a case on their part that, for example, exclusion from the business was justified.

Exclusion from a company can lead to a degree of paranoia and assumptions being made about what is happening in the company on the basis of what is often scant evidence. Minority shareholders should be cautious about leaping to conclusions and those advising them careful about advancing claims of wrongdoing, without having the evidence to back it up.

Investigation and verification are key steps in the process of investigating the strength of any claim. Unfair prejudice claims can often be based upon cumulative incidents but if these are exaggerated or have gained a greater significance in the mind of the minority shareholder than can be objectively justified then such a claim can rapidly unravel.

A key part of this investigation should be to get a good feel for the value of the shares in dispute. This needs to be considered as part of the commerciality of any action as well as having a direct impact on the availability of third-party funding (see below). Note that the estimated value will in any event usually have to be stated to the court at an early point in proceedings. The failure to give a minority shareholder the essential information they require in order to assess the value of their shares is unlikely to endear the majority shareholders to the court and may itself be an example of unfair prejudice in some cases.

A very important consideration is whether or not any discount will be applied to the valuation of the minority shareholding. This is considered in more detail in chapter 12. An early assessment should be made as to whether there are circumstances which may mean that the "normal rules" on valuation will not apply.

A particular pressure point in very small companies, particularly 50 / 50 businesses can be the impact of informing the company's bank that there is a dispute. In many cases this can result in the bank freezing the company's account until the bank is certain that instructions for payment are properly authorised. No bank wishes to be in the middle of a shareholder dispute and potentially accused of aiding one shareholder / director to improperly extract funds. This can be a high-risk tactic on the part of the excluded shareholder as it can severely damage the company and if not justified may count against that shareholder in any litigation.

Another way of applying pressure where a shareholder has been excluded from their role as an employee of the company is to bring employment tribunal proceedings against the company claiming unfair dismissal or wrongful dismissal. This may be embarrassing for the other shareholders thus encouraging settlement. It may also result in the payment of a sum of money which can be the fighting fund for pursuing a petition.

However, a note of caution, whilst the findings of a tribunal are not directly binding on a Judge in a petition there is the risk of adverse findings in the tribunal as to the evidence of certain matters or the truthfulness of a witnesses evidence that may rebound in later proceedings.

A further point to note is that there is authority that a wrongful dismissal claim (i.e. a contractual one rather than a statutory one) can be brought within an unfair prejudice petition thus avoiding the need for multiple proceedings (*Stanley Wootliff v Martin Rushton-Turner & 6 Ors [2016] EWHC 2802 (Ch)*)

Advisers should also assess the reverse risk of a claim coming from the company (see chapter 9) and factor this into the overall merits of pursuing the case / settling it. Note that this will ordinarily have to be way of separate proceedings as the court would not generally have jurisdiction to hear it within a s.994 petition.

Although the majority shareholders do hold most of the cards, if the grounds for unfair prejudice can be established and an action brought then at that point the dynamics change. From then on, in the absence of doing a deal, the majority shareholders must potentially fight on at high personal risk and expense. If they want to make an offer of settlement, for example for the purchase of the minority's shares, then ordinarily this will have to be "plus costs" in order to be effective. For the reasons stated elsewhere in this book, taking a s.994 or s.122(1)(g) petition to trial is a high risk for both parties but in light of the potential financial downside for the majority shareholders it can be a higher overall risk for them.

This can be a product of how the claim is funded. Claims with good merits which have sufficient value can attract third party funding and lawyers willing to take them on a contingency basis (no win / no fee or no win / reduced fee). This can make the upfront costs of the case affordable for petitioners. In addition petitioners can often obtain after the event (ATE) insurance to cover the costs risks of losing. This is rarely available to respondents to petitions.

Such funding / insurance does not come cheap and the economics in relation any case will need to be carefully considered. Such costs are not recoverable from the losing party, unlike standard legal costs. They will need to be picked up by the petitioner out of their winnings. This has an impact on the timing and dynamics of settlement discussions. Once a third-party funding agreement / ATE policy is signed up then the providers will be entitled to a return on their investment / premium which ordinarily increases as the litigation progresses. This means that the further the litigation goes, the more a petitioner needs to recover in order to get a reasonable return from any overall settlement amount

This needs to be borne in mind as much by the respondents to the petition as the petitioner. Settlement at an early stage may be considerably cheaper and it may get to a point where a fully funded petitioner has nothing to lose but see it through to a final hearing.

CHAPTER ELEVEN

DECEASED SHAREHOLDERS AND BANKRUPT SHAREHOLDERS

Unless held jointly, in which case it will pass to the other holder(s) by survivorship, a deceased shareholder's shares will pass under the terms of their will to their named beneficiaries or the appropriate parties on an intestacy. This is subject to any provisions to the contrary in the Articles of Association or a shareholders' agreement.

If a shareholder is made bankrupt then their shares form part of their estate which passes to their Trustee in Bankruptcy.

All standard Articles of Association contain provisions relating to the transmission of shares on death or bankruptcy. Bespoke Articles of Association often have more detailed provisions about what will happen in these circumstances.

The Model Articles (Article 27) and Table A (Regulations 29 – 31 in the most recent versions) provide that the shares may be transferred to either the transmittee i.e. the personal representatives of the deceased shareholder (e.g. the executors of a Will) or their Trustee in Bankruptcy, or at the direction of the transmittee, to a third party (e.g. the ultimate beneficiaries).

The directors may require evidence of entitlement to be provided and on death this is likely to be a Grant of Probate or Letters of Administration. Although there is no strict requirement to wait for these to be obtained the court has affirmed (see for example *Kings Court Trust Ltd v Lancashire Cleaning Services Ltd [2017] EWHC 1096 (Ch)*) that the directors are normally entitled to wait for these before registering any transmission of shares.

Pending the registration of the transfer the transmittee has the same rights as the original holder (e.g. to dividends) but has no right to vote at a general meeting or on a written shareholders resolution.

On the death of a shareholder in a family business the continuing shareholders may therefore find themselves with their former shareholder's partner or children as significant shareholders in the company. These parties will be entitled to all the rights attached to the shares whilst not necessarily playing a part in the running of the business, although they may well assert a right to actively take part.

For this reason the existing shareholders / directors may decline to agree to register any transfer in the absence of, for example a Grant of Probate (which can take some time to obtain) and in the interim use the fact that the personal representatives have no voting rights to force through changes in the business, including amending the Articles of Association. If these changes are not bona fide for the business but are instead designed to benefit the existing shareholders then the new shareholders may have a right of action under s.994 which at sub-paragraph (2) confirms;

> *"The provisions of this Part apply to a person who is not a member of a company but to whom shares in the company have been transferred or transmitted by operation of law as they apply to a member of a company."*

Accordingly a Trustee in Bankruptcy can petition the court under s.994. The position is slightly different under s.122(1)(g) as by virtue of s.124 of the Insolvency Act 1986 a Trustee in Bankruptcy (but not e.g. personal representatives) must hold the shares in their own name for 6 months before they can petition.

Looking at it from the other side of the coin on the death of a shareholder, the new shareholders may expect that they will be able to simply realise the financial value of their shares, but if there is no mechanism compelling the other shareholders to purchase them then there is no right to this. Even if the shareholders are prepared to, and can afford to, buy the shares, if it is a minority holding then it is likely that the value of the shareholding will be materially discounted to take this into account.

On bankruptcy, the Trustee in Bankruptcy will have an obligation to realise the financial value of the shareholding for the benefit of all creditors. Given the nature of family businesses it is likely that the only purchaser of the shares will / can be one or more of the existing shareholders.

This can cause problems if only one shareholder has the funds to acquire the shares and this will give them a controlling interest which they did not have previously.

It can be seen that death or bankruptcy of a shareholder can cause significant structural problems within a family business and as a result many shareholder disputes arise in relation to inherited shares. As discussed above, a well drafted shareholders' agreement or bespoke Articles of Association can head off these problems by providing mechanisms, such as compulsory purchase or surrender provisions which take effect on the death or bankruptcy of a shareholder.

One specific problem which can arise is where there is just one director / shareholder formally appointed in a business. In these circumstances, if standard Articles of Association are in place there is an intractable problem. The personal representatives cannot vote to appoint a new director until they are registered as members. The only person who can formally add a new member to the company's register of members is a director (or company secretary if there is one). The solution is to apply to the court under s.125 of the Companies Act 2006 for rectification (see chapter 7).

It is a slightly inelegant solution as it requires a degree of stretching the meaning of that section. It was approved in *Kings Court Trust Ltd v Lancashire Cleaning Services Ltd [2017] EWHC 1096 (Ch)* under s.125(a) where there was an urgent need to appoint a director to prevent the business from failing and it was therefore held appropriate to consider all the circumstances. It was approved in a slightly different way in the case of *Williams v Russell Price Farm Services [2020] EWHC 1088 (Ch)* where the Judge held that under s.125(b) there was "unnecessary delay" in waiting for probate enabling the court to make an order that the register of members be amended to substitute the personal representatives of the deceased shareholder.

CHAPTER TWELVE

VALUING THE COMPANY / SHAREHOLDING

The valuation of companies has an undeserved reputation as being something of a dark art. However, at the most basic level a company is simply worth what somebody will pay for it (either actually or theoretically) and there are various tried and tested ways that accountants will approach this exercise.

These valuation methods will depend upon the nature of the business and, for example, whether it is a going concern. A detailed analysis is outside the scope of this book but the standard methods of valuation are:

- The price / earnings approach where future maintainable earnings (usually by reference to EBITDA) are calculated subject to various adjustments and then a multiple (reflecting potential future growth and risk) applied to reach what can be described as the enterprise value of the company. This is most appropriate where the purpose of the business is primarily to generate profits.

- The net asset approach, appropriate where the business is either essentially asset holding only or no longer a going concern.

- The discounted cash flow approach, involving estimating future cash-flows and converting to a current value by use of a discount rate reflecting anticipated risk. This is more suitable for substantial or high cash generative companies.

- The dividend yield approach, arriving at a value based on the estimated flow of dividends to be paid going forward multiplied by a suitable capitalisation. This is most suitable for a small shareholding where the value lies principally in the income from the shares.

Each of these valuation methods will then be subject to adjustments to reflect the factual situation in relation to the company in question. Some of the principal areas where adjustments will be made are:

- Capital expenditure – either if this is likely to be required in the future or has been recently incurred and has not yet delivered the anticipated benefits.
- Surplus assets – if they are genuinely surplus to the requirements of the business then it may be appropriate to value them separately and in addition.
- Surplus debts or liabilities – if they are exceptional or outside normal trading then it may be appropriate to reflect that in the valuation.

Where the company holds significant assets such as a property then a separate expert valuation of such assets will need to be obtained. An accountant's view is still likely to be necessary to come to a view on the overall valuation having regard to the potential costs of realising the assets including tax liabilities.

A full-blown expert valuation for a court case will cost many tens of thousands of pounds but that is not necessarily what is required at the initial stage of a dispute. What may be needed in the first instance is a ballpark figure that can be used as the basis of an initial risk analysis and also potentially form the basis of settlement discussions.

This early risk analysis is important as there are dangers associated with taking the value of the shares as read and focusing instead just on the merits of the claim. This danger can be accentuated by the split nature of s.994 litigation (see chapter 14 for a cautionary tale in this respect).

In this latter respect, some disputes are really just about "how much". Deep down the parties realise that one or other has to leave and it is simply a question of how much the other will take / pay for the shares. In these cases it can sometimes be agreed that an accountant will act jointly for the parties to value the shares. The parties will each pay half of the cost of getting a valuation and either agree to be bound by the valuation or less formally just use the valuation obtained as the starting point for discussions.

If an agreed process is not possible and settlement is not otherwise reached then ultimately a Judge will have to make decision as to the value of the shares. This has two parts to it, the value of the company as a whole (i.e. the entirety of the shares) and the value of the particular shares in question. The Judge will be heavily reliant on expert evidence and if there is no consensus between opposing experts may have to make a binary choice to simply prefer one expert's opinion over another. If any case does get to this stage (and it is relatively rare for them to do so) then the quality of expert evidence being presented will be key to success.

An example of how a Judge will approach competing evidence in relation to valuation can be found in the case of *Re. Campbell Irvine (Holdings) Ltd [2006] EWHC 1875 (Ch)* and the judgment of Mr Justice Blackburne. The Judge sets out his thinking in relation to the competing positions of the experts on each side and how he steered a path between them to arrive at the ultimate valuation.

The aim of any Judge will be to arrive at a fair outcome and to achieve this may require adjustments to be made to the valuation or dictate the terms on which it should be carried out. Some examples of this can be found in the cases referred to below in this chapter but possible judicial interventions can include:

- Adding back the value of money improperly taken out of a company (including that improperly spent on legal fees);
- Adding back a sum to reflect excessive remuneration;
- Adjusting to reflect losses caused by the unfairly prejudicial behaviour itself;
- Requiring the assumption on the part of the valuer that the act of unfair prejudice had not occurred;

- Hindsight – indicating whether events or matters which occurred after the date on which the shares are being valued ought to be taken into account (the general rule being that they should not – *Shah v Shah [2011] EWHC 1902*).

It should not be forgotten that the scope of s.996 is very wide and the remedies can therefore include an element of compensation for wider losses suffered by the petitioner.

It is also necessary, whether a valuation is being done by agreement or by order of the court, to understand the key legal as well as the accountancy principles which are relevant.

Discount or no discount?

One core principle which is sometimes not understood by minority shareholders in family businesses is that that the starting point for any commercial valuation of a minority holding is that there will be discount to reflect that it is a minority holding. The valuation will not therefore be a pro rata valuation. This reflects the fact that in the open market any purchaser would discount the amount paid for a minority holding. The level of discounts vary from sector to sector and on the type of assets held by the company but can be significant.

This discounting to reflect "market" or "commercial" valuation of shares is a concept acknowledged by the court although its application as a general rule to be applied has been judicially challenged. The Judge in *Re Blue Index Ltd [2014] EWHC 2680 (Ch)* expressed the view in that case that the starting point for all companies (not just quasi-partnership companies) when granting relief under s.996 was that it should be a non-discounted valuation. This approach has been approved in some subsequent cases but it is not clear that it has replaced the traditional assumption that a discount will normally be appropriate when valuing a company that is not a quasi-partnership company.

In "quasi-partnership" companies, which will be the case for many family companies, the normal rule is different. In such cases shares will usually be valued without a discount (in other words, pro rata to the value of the entire shareholding). The case usually cited in support of this proposition is *Re. Bird Precision Bellows Ltd [1984] Ch.419*, the judgment in which was affirmed by the Court of Appeal. The often quoted passage from the judgment of Nourse J which has gained the status of a general rule is as follows:

> *"I would expect that in a majority of cases where purchase orders are made under [s.994] in relation to quasi-partnerships the vendor is unwilling in the sense that the sale has been forced upon him. Usually he will be a minority shareholder whose interests have been unfairly prejudiced by the manner in which the affairs of the company have been conducted by the majority. On the assumption that the unfair prejudice has made it no longer tolerable for him to retain his interest in the company, a sale of his shares will invariably be his only practical way out short of a winding-up. In that kind of case it seems to me that it would not merely not be fair, but most unfair, that he should be bought out on the fictional basis applicable to a free election to sell his shares in accordance with the company's articles of association, or indeed on any other basis which involved a discounted price. In my judgement the correct course would be to fix the price pro rata according to the value of the shares as a whole and without any discount, as being the only fair method of compensating an unwilling vendor of the equivalent of a partnership share."*

Given the financial impact of potential discounts, the question of whether a company is or is not a quasi-partnership therefore takes on a particular importance when it comes to valuation.

The court can always choose not to follow the normal rule, reflecting the broad powers it has under s.996 to do justice in any particular case. Thus, where not applying a discount would result in an unjustified windfall for the minority shareholder the court may choose to reflect the true commercial value of a minority holding instead.

The court may also find that a discount should be applied where the petitioner has been partially the author of their own misfortune, where it would be unfair, even in a quasi-partnership company, to require the majority shareholders to purchase at a pro rata value. This was a situation envisaged by Mr Justice Nourse himself in the Bird Precision Bellows case.

Other adjustments may also be made to any valuation to ensure that it is a fair one. This may include, for example, adding back in the value of excessive remuneration paid to a majority shareholder or taking into account other wrongful acts that have reduced the value of the company. As a result, even where a company is not a quasi-partnership, there may be good arguments to made to increase the valuation of a minority shareholding to reflect the wider factual context.

Examples of how the court has approached valuation on this basis and where the normal rules have been departed from can be found in the following cases.

In the case of *CF Booth Ltd [2017] EWHC 457 (Ch)*, whilst this was a family company, it was not held to be a "quasi-partnership". In this case the Judge held that a "fair" valuation of the minority's shareholding required a 33% discount to reflect the minority status.

The better news for the successful minority family members was that the court ordered that in valuing the company on a balance sheet basis, the excessive remuneration that it was found to have been paid to the majority shareholder should be added back in when arriving at a value.

A creative approach can also be found in the case of *Estera Trust (Jersey) Limited v Singh & Ors [2018] EWHC 1715 (Ch)*, which was in essence a dispute between two brothers in a large family business. Again, it was held that it was not a quasi-partnership company. However, the Judge emphasised that it was not a binary choice between the undiscounted value and the commercial or market value. The Judge cited with approval a passage from the judgement in another case (*Re Eurofinance Group Ltd [2001] B.C.C. 551*) as follows:

> *"I think that when arriving at a 'fair value' in the absence of a market it is necessary to assume that the notional sale is taking place between the actual participants in the transaction, since the whole purpose of the valuation is to be fair as between the parties."*

The Judge decided that this principle was not limited to the situation (as in the Eurofinance case) where there was no market for the shares) and the court was therefore entitled to take into account the "marriage value" of the shares where relevant in relation to any company. Thus the valuation in this case was required to take into account the particular value to the majority shareholder acquiring them.

Another case of interest is *Re. Sunrise Radio Ltd [2009] EWHC 2893 (Ch)* where a non-discounted valuation was ordered in relation to a company that was not a quasi-partnership. The Judge lists a number of factors which lead to his conclusion that this was the fair outcome in all the circumstances of that case. Valuation was a particularly contentious issue in this case, leading to several spin off judgments and appeals.

The date of valuation

Another factor that may significantly affect the amount paid for the shares is the date on which the shares are to be valued. This can have a significant impact on the overall valuation and the court has a wide discretion to determine the appropriate date having regard to all the circumstances. The most usual date for the valuation is the date on which the shares are ordered to be purchased (see the case of *Profinance Trust SA v Gladstone [2001] EWCA Civ 1031*).

The timing of the valuation was considered in some detail in the case of *Re K R Hardy Estates Ltd [2014] EWHC 4001 (Ch)*. A number of different points in time were considered as being the possible points at which to value the minority shareholder's shares. These included:

- The date the unfair prejudice occurred
- The date on which the value of the shares was adversely affected
- The date the Petition was issued
- The date on which the order for sale was made

After reviewing the possible dates in the context of the facts of this particular case the conclusion was that the fairest date was the date on which the order was made, although it was left open to adjust the value to reflect the direct loss which the particular shareholder had suffered as the result of salary / benefits being withdrawn in the interim.

Another example of an earlier valuation date being ordered can be found in the Eurofinance case referred to above. Here it was held that the petitioner had unduly delayed and it would be unfair for them to benefit from an uplift in the value of the business during the course of that delay.

The reverse reason for an earlier valuation date was identified in the case of *Re. Foundry Miniatures Ltd [2017] EWHC 889 (Ch)* where it was held that the way that the business was run had changed significantly since the petitioner had been (unfairly) expelled from management and there was evidence that non-commercial considerations to the benefit of the majority shareholders were holding sway. In light of this there was a clear risk that the petitioner's shares were devalued unfairly since his departure and it would therefore be just to value them at that date and not later.

Similar reasons lead to an early valuation date to the benefit of the petitioners in the CF Booth case. Here it was held that the respondents' resistance of the claim had effectively left the petitioners locked in to a loss-making company which the court they should be entitled to leave. On this basis they should not have to bear any of the loss incurred since the petition date.

What these cases illustrate is that whilst there is flexibility as to when a shareholding is valued the court tends to the view that a going concern ought to be valued at the date on which it was ordered to be purchased. If another date is proposed then there will need to be some justification for this, which means that it will generally be necessary to persuade the court that it would be unfair to the petitioner (or the respondents) for the shares to be valued on that date.

By way of another example, if the respondent to a petition deliberately takes steps to damage a company such that by the time the order for sale of the shares is made it is worth considerably less than when the unfair prejudice started, it is likely that the court will say that an earlier valuation date is appropriate.

However, if the company is worth less as a result of external factors such as changes in the market then the court is unlikely to order an earlier valuation date merely because that date favours a meritorious petitioner.

In summary, the question of how shares should be valued for either an agreed exit or in terms of assessing the likely outcome in the event of a court ordered purchase is potentially the subject of considerable argument and hence a high degree of uncertainty which should be taken into account by all parties to a dispute.

CHAPTER THIRTEEN

THE LITIGATION PROCESS

There are some aspects of the litigation process in shareholder actions which are different from ordinary commercial litigation which means some elephant traps for the unwary general practitioner. Some the main things to look out for are highlighted in this chapter.

The first point to note is that claims of unfair prejudice under s.994 and for just and equitable winding up under s.122(1)(g) are commenced by way of petition in the Business & Property Courts rather than by a claim form. Derivative actions however commence by way of a claim form. Most such actions are commenced in the High Court.

There is no specific pre-action protocol in relation to any of these actions but the Practice Direction on Pre-Action Conduct should generally be complied with. This means that there should be pre-action correspondence consisting at the very least of a detailed letter before action and a full response, with key documents being exchanged.

Unfair prejudice petitions

The parties to the petition will be:

- the shareholder seeking a remedy (the petitioner);
- the shareholders (or other party, e.g. a former shareholder) whose actions are complained of;
- any other shareholders whose interests may be affected;
- the company (together the respondents).

As noted in chapter 9, the company is an essential respondent but effectively a nominal one. In small companies, all shareholders will in practice be made parties to the petition although some may take no active part.

The Civil Procedure Rules (CPR) are augmented by the Companies (Unfair Prejudice Applications) Proceedings Rules 2009, which amongst other things prescribe the form of the petition.

As noted in chapter 6, a petition in relation to unfair prejudice can seek in the alternative the winding up of the company on just and equitable grounds but this practice is discouraged.

The petition can be in a very short form, akin to a claim form, with a more detailed document (the points of claim) being served later. However, the usual practice is to serve a detailed document which effectively incorporates the points of claim.

On presentation of the petition at court a first hearing is fixed by the court (known as the 'return day') at which directions will be given. This was traditionally endorsed on the petition itself, which then had to be served on all respondents at least 14 days before the return day.

In practice the court will usually of its own motion make preliminary directions dealing with certain matters prior to the hearing. This order for directions will confirm the return day and must be served at the same time as the petition. The preliminary directions can include:

- That the petition should stand as points of claim;
- Points of defence to be filed by a certain date;
- Points of reply to be filed by a certain date;
- Directions re. costs budgets
- Directions re. disclosure (including the applicability of the Disclosure Pilot)
- A direction to provide a non-binding indication of the value of the shares in issue in the petition.

The return day will then effectively be a costs case management hearing fixing further directions to take the matter to trial. Specific issues which are considered at such a hearing in relation to petitions include:

- Whether the petition needs to be served on any interested party;
- Whether the petition should be advertised. The 2009 rules referred to above require that the petition should not be notified to third parties until the return day (to prevent the petition being used to apply improper pressure on the company). The normal order made is that the petition should not be advertised.

Petitions have also traditionally been subject to more active case management than ordinary claims but as the CPR has been developed this distinction has become less significant. Nevertheless, the court is more inclined in such cases to look at the underlying merits and at an early stage, even on its own motion, strike out an unmeritorious petition. The circumstances where this can occur include:

- Where there are obvious technical issues with the petition, for example the petitioner is not a member;
- If the evidence being advanced could not properly sustain an allegation of unfair prejudice;
- Where a petitioner has refused a reasonable offer from the respondents to purchase their shares (see chapter 8 for more details).

Subject to the above petitions will proceed to trial in the same way as any other litigation.

One other point to note is that it has become usual for there to be a split trial. The first part (the liability hearing) limited to establishing whether there has been unfair prejudice and if so whether a buyout order should be made. Only in the event of the petitioner succeeding will there be a second hearing (the quantum hearing) which will decide the value of the shares. In practice the second hearing is often not required as faced with a finding of unfair prejudice the parties will often negotiate and agree a buyout.

Just & equitable winding up petitions

The parties to such a petition are the same as for an unfair prejudice petition.

These are treated as insolvency proceedings and therefore the CPR apply but subject to the Insolvency Rules 1986 ('the Insolvency Rules').

It should also be noted that by virtue of s.127 of the Insolvency Act 1986, unless the court orders otherwise, any disposition of the company's property made after the presentation of the petition is void. This in practice means that the company will not be able to carry out its business unless such an order is made (for example, the company's bank will normally freeze all accounts on notice of such a petition).

Such a situation is not normally in any party's interests and there is a mechanism provided to avoid this in Practice Direction 49B – Order under s.127 of the Insolvency Act 1986.

Paragraph 2 requires that:

> *Whenever a winding up order is asked for in a contributory's petition, the petition must state whether the petitioner consents or objects to an order under s.127 of the Insolvency Act 1986 ('a s.127 order') in the standard form. If he objects, the written evidence in support must contain a short statement of his reasons.*

The standard form of order is set out in paragraph 7:

> *Section 127 Order – Standard Form:*
>
> *(Title etc.)*
>
> *ORDER that notwithstanding the presentation of the said Petition*
>
> *(1) payments made into or out of the bank accounts of the Company in the ordinary course of business of the Company and*

> *(2) dispositions of the property of the Company made in the ordinary course of its business for proper value between the date of presentation of the Petition and the date of judgment on the Petition or further order in the meantime*
>
> *shall not be void by virtue of the provisions of section 127 of the Insolvency Act 1986 in the event of an Order for the winding up of the Company being made on the said Petition provided that (the relevant bank) shall be under no obligation to verify for itself whether any transaction through the company's bank accounts is in the ordinary course of business, or that it represents full market value for the relevant transaction .*

The petitioner can agree a modified version of the order as per paragraph 3:

> *If the petitioner objects to a s.127 order in the standard form but consents to such an order in a modified form, the petition must set out in the form of order to which he consents, and the written evidence in support must contain a short statement of his reasons for seeking the modification.*

The effect of such consent by the petitioner is set out in paragraph 5:

> *If the petition contains a statement that the petitioner consents to a s.127 order, whether in the standard or a modified form, the Registrar shall without further enquiry make an order in such form at the first hearing unless an order to the contrary has been made by the Judge in the meantime.*

In the event that the petitioner does not consent to the standard order for any reason then paragraph 6 confirms the right of the company to apply for relief:

> *If the petition contains a statement that the petitioner objects to a s.127 order in the standard form, the company may apply (in the case of urgency, without notice) to the Judge for an order.*

As with an unfair prejudice petition the court will fix a return day for the first hearing and may make directions of its own motion. Only the company is formally required to be served with the petition but usual practice is to serve on all respondents.

Specific items to be considered on the return day include the question of advertisement as unlike creditor's petitions there is no formal provision in the Insolvency Rules for the advertisement in the Gazette. In most cases an order will be made that no advertisement should be made until further order or until after the final hearing.

On the return day directions will also normally be made to take the matter to a final hearing. There is not normally a split trial.

Derivative actions

These proceed as normal actions under the CPR but are subject to their own specific rules and practice direction – CPR 19.9 – 19.9F and PD 19C which should be referred to in this respect.

The parties to the claim will be:

- the shareholder seeking a remedy (the claimant);
- the shareholders (or other party, e.g. a former shareholder) whose actions are complained of; and
- the company (together the defendants).

Normal CPR rules apply with regard to service and acknowledgment of service. Particulars of Claim need to be filed promptly together with the application notice requesting permission.

CPR19.9 sets out the requirement and mechanism for obtaining the permission of the court to proceed (and see also chapter 7).

A cautionary tale with regard to costs

As discussed in chapter 4, shareholder disputes by their nature tend to be evidence heavy. This means that both the disclosure process and production of witness statements can be labour intensive, time consuming and hence very expensive in terms of legal costs.

This is likely to be brought home to all parties at an early stage in the costs budgeting process where this applies. As noted elsewhere, this means that this is often high stakes litigation for the parties. The tendency for there to be a split trial between merits and quantum in s.994 petitions can also increase those costs and the ultimate uncertainty of outcome. In this respect the following case provides a cautionary tale.

The petition under s.994 in *Ashdown v Griffin [2018] EWCA Civ 1793* concerned a company promoting "AdBins", which were cigarette bins outside pubs and clubs with advertising on. The company had ended up with only one real client, being the taxi company Addison Lee and the majority shareholder and directors were linked to that company.

As a matter of fact it was found that the company was being run for benefit of Addison Lee and to the detriment of other shareholders. At first instance the court ordered a buy-out of shares with no minority discount, an apparently resounding victory for the petitioning shareholders.

However, at the hearing on quantum the shares were held to be practically worthless. Nonetheless, as the victors the minority shareholders were awarded their costs (with a payment on account of £150,000). The first instance Judge chose not to give much weight to offers that had been made by the majority shareholder and criticised his conduct. He appealed.

The Court of Appeal overturned the costs order. In their judgment, as the value of the shares was zero the petitioners could not be considered successful. They had been seeking substantial sums for their shares and they had failed. The Court of Appeal judges also placed more weight on the costs inclusive offers made by the majority shareholder and concluded that his behaviour (arrogance, intransigence and "utter contempt" for the petitioners) did not mean that he should be penalised as it had not actually caused the proceedings to be conducted in an inappropriate way.

The victorious petitioners were thus ordered to pay all of the costs of the action.

Another cautionary tale

Finally, a salutary lesson for legal advisers about what can go wrong in shareholder litigation is given by this professional negligence case – *[2021] EWHC 22 (Ch) Percy v Merriman White.*

There were alleged to be a series of errors on the part of a litigation solicitor in relation to advising on the appropriate course of action in a shareholder dispute. These errors were compounded by inadequate advice found to have been received from counsel who was apparently not that experienced in relation to shareholders disputes.

The result was a disastrous and expensive derivative action launched on behalf of the client that fell at the first hurdle. The client sued the solicitors who made a payment to the client to settle the claim. In the case cited, the solicitors then sought a contribution from counsel, which was duly granted. The Judge's comments on the failures in the process of advising on a course of action in a shareholders' dispute and also on the importance of properly analysing the merits of offers of settlement (and whether they should be accepted) makes illuminating reading.

CHAPTER FOURTEEN

CASE STUDIES

The importance of case law in relation to shareholders disputes should not be underestimated.

Both section 994 and section 122(g)(1) require a knowledge of the underlying case law in order to understand how they will operate in practice. For this reason shareholder litigation in relation to family companies in particular can contain elephant traps which the non-specialist can easily fall into.

The following four case studies, mostly involving family businesses, provide examples of how the court approaches these cases (and also what can go wrong with such cases). The judgments in these cases all merit detailed reading in the event of a case with similar facts as they provide a good guide to how the courts approach the issues and what elements need particular attention.

Re. Westshield Ltd – sibling rivalry and the importance of fairness

The case of *Re. Westshield [2019] EWHC 115 (Ch)* is a reminder that a party seeking relief under s.994 must establish that (a) they have suffered prejudice and (b) that the prejudice is unfair. It is the question of whether what has happened is unfair that is often the most critical element.

As discussed above, two factors that are regularly considered in this respect are whether the company is what is known in shorthand as a "quasi-partnership" and the petitioner's own conduct.

The first is relevant in terms of deciding whether what would otherwise be a lawful exercise of rights in fact amounts to a breach of some understanding or legitimate expectation on the part of the petitioner. The second factor can affect whether or not what has happened is unfair or, just as importantly, what remedy is appropriate.

Both these elements are often centre stage in disputes within family companies. In particular, the added emotional element of a family at war can mean that both sides behave badly requiring the court to exercise fine judgment. The Westshield case is a useful example of how the court can approach these issues.

What was the background?

The petitioners were siblings who were all shareholders in the family business, Westshield Ltd, which had been set up by their parents.

The respondent was their brother who had effective control of the company. Two of the petitioners worked in the company at the material time. Following an incident in which these two petitioners sought to gain access to their brother's emails, the respondent dismissed them both and effectively excluded them from the company.

This had followed several years in which relationships between the siblings had become increasingly strained, primarily arising from differences of opinion with regard to how the company should be run.

The petitioners then sought relief under s.994. They sought an order that the respondent should be required to purchase their shares in the company on a pro rata basis (i.e. without any discount to reflect the fact that these were minority shares).

What did the court decide?

The parties in the dispute made numerous allegations and counter-allegations ranging from assertions of bad behaviour thorough to serious allegations of fraud.

The Judge, His Honour Judge Eyre QC, had to decide:

- was the company a quasi-partnership at the material time?
- was the petitioner's conduct unfairly prejudicial?
- if so, what relief was appropriate?

In relation to the first of these issues the Judge carried out a helpful review of the authorities on the question of when a company is a quasi-partnership. He concluded that in summary he was looking for those characteristics in the relationship between the shareholders which might make it unfair for a majority shareholder to exercise what would otherwise be their lawful rights. This is not always an easy exercise in family companies as it can involve untangling legitimate expectations from those which are not based on shared understandings but rather on historic family grievances or contradictory points of view.

In the Westfield case there was a particular issue as to whether there could be a quasi-partnership if the required understandings did not extend to all shareholders. After a careful consideration of the authorities the Judge concluded that this would not preclude a finding that the company was a quasi-partnership.

The Judge also considered the nature of the test to be applied with regard to fairness or unfairness. He emphasised that it was an objective test on the basis that it was by reference to principle and authority rather by reference to what any party believed. Further, he emphasised the need for the test to be undertaken by reference to all the relevant circumstances and background.

Counsel for the petitioners had argued that there needed to be causal connection between any bad behaviour on the part of the petitioners and the prejudice they had suffered in order for that behaviour to make what was otherwise unfair, fair. The Judge was not willing to be constrained in this respect and in any event pointed out that such behaviour would be highly relevant to what remedy was appropriate.

Finally, the Judge noted the importance of breaches of fiduciary duty, which would generally equate to unfairly prejudicial conduct. However, these must also be considered in the light of all the circumstances and in particular whether there had been any acquiescence by the complaining party.

Having then reviewed the factual evidence the Judge noted that in the course of evidence one of the petitioners gave a false account in relation to his involvement with other companies and that he did not consider any of the three principal parties as being reliable witnesses.

Against this background the Judge concluded as follows:

- Having unpicked the complicated history of the company, he found that there was a family understanding that did constrain the respondent in the exercise of his powers.

- This was not changed by subsequent commercial events and the involvement of third-party investors.

- A company owned by the respondent had acquired assets in breach of an understanding that these would be acquired by Westfield. This was unfairly prejudicial conduct by the respondent.

- Contrary to the evidence of the principal petitioners, they had offered an IT consultant money to wrongfully access the respondent's emails and this was improper conduct on their part.

- As a result, and looking at things in the round, the Judge found that their exclusion from the company did not amount to unfair prejudice.

- With regard to the unfair prejudice on the part of the respondent that had been identified (in relation to the acquisition of assets) the Judge found that petitioners had acquiesced as evidenced by the fact that they had known about the matter for some years and failed to take any action or even raise any significant complaint. Accordingly, this did not entitle them to any relief either.

As a result, the Judge declined to make an order requiring the respondent to acquire the shares of his siblings. Thus, unless they came to an agreement the siblings remained locked together in the family company having spent years of their lives, and lots of their money, on an ultimately fruitless legal battle.

In summary, bad behaviour by the petitioners in this case had made what was a breach of their legitimate expectations nevertheless fair, and their acquiescence in bad behaviour by the respondent had denied them any remedy in that respect either.

Re. Weatherley Fencing Contractors Ltd – legitimate expectations?

The case of *Weatherley Fencing Contractors Ltd [2018] EWHC 3201 (Ch)* also considered the behaviour of the petitioner but also took a close look at family understandings about a how a company should be run and how far these should be enforced.

Family owned companies are often subject to understandings and agreements about how they will operate. These understandings can be quite informal and often not written down. As discussed in chapter 5 they can amount to "legitimate expectations" which go above and beyond shareholders strict rights under the articles of association.

Examples of expectations that are often seen in family businesses include:

- Shareholders will have a role in the strategic management of the business,
- Dividends will be paid regardless of an individual shareholder's contribution to the business,
- Family shareholders will be entitled to a job within the company,
- Certain benefits, such as private healthcare, will be available to family shareholders.

If these expectations reflect genuine mutual understandings or informal agreements and they are breached then shareholders may be entitled to seek a remedy from the court on the grounds that they are being unfairly prejudiced.

What was the background?

Weatherley Fencing was a small private company which suffered the tragic loss at an early age of its main director, the son of the founder. The petitioner was the deceased director's wife, who had worked in the company as his PA.

It was accepted by all that there was an agreement that the company was run for the benefit of the family. The petitioner asserted that it went beyond this and it was understood that family members would always have a job and benefits such as private healthcare paid for by the company and that ownership of shares would pass down the two main branches of the family (of which she now represented one).

Following her husband's death relations soured with the other family members in the company, most of whom were employed in the company.

Her complaints included:

- her exclusion from the company
- the denial of a job
- the directors' refusal to give her information
- non-payment of dividends
- the attempted imposition of new articles of association allowing the directors to refuse to register any transfer of shares to her

There was also a complicated claim with regard to the historic transfer of some company property and what should have happened to the proceeds of sale.

There were various counter-allegations about her behaviour, including that she shredded company documents and made secret recordings (the latter used in support of her case).

What did the court decide?

The Judge's findings can be summarised as follows:

- Whilst the company was run for the benefit of the family this was more in the way of family members having opportunities rather than absolute entitlements. Benefits, including a job were not automatic.

- There was no agreement binding the father and mother to leaving their shares a certain way.

- There was no unfair prejudice as a result of the property transfer

- There was a breakdown of mutual trust and confidence, but the petitioner's actions with the secret recordings and shredding of documents was at the heart of it. She was therefore to some extent the author of her own misfortune.

- During the course of the petition open offers had been made with regard to dividends and with regard to rectifying the articles (actions which were unfairly prejudicial) and to purchase the petitioners shares. These had largely rectified those matters which were arguably unfairly prejudicial.

- The Judge did not accept there was any likelihood of such unfairly prejudicial actions being repeated.

In light of these findings the petition was dismissed. The key lessons from this case are twofold.

First, understandings / expectations may not simply flow down through the generations. In other words, the children or spouse of a child of the founding shareholder may find that these expectations do not apply to them. They are outside of the initial circle of trust.

Secondly, the behaviour of the shareholder bringing the claim will be looked at closely and the weaker the claim for legitimate expectations is, the more likely it is that it will be possible to justify not meeting those expectations on commercial grounds or in light of that shareholders behaviour.

For example, it may be held that an expectation of a job within the company by a second or third generation family member can be legitimately ignored if they lack any talent or if they have behaved badly.

In summary, understandings between family shareholders, even if not formally documented, are important and will potentially be given weight by the court in unfair prejudice proceedings. However, the less well documented they are, and the further from the centre of things the shareholder is, the harder it will be to prove that there is an unfair breach of such understandings. In this context the behaviour of the petitioner will be of particular importance and may well tip the balance against them.

Re Sprintroom Ltd – a different take on bad behaviour

A counterpoint to the above two cases is that of *Re. Sprintroom Ltd [2019] EWCA Civ 932 (Ch)*, which has already been looked at for different reasons in chapter 8. In this case the Court of Appeal upheld the Judge's decision that the petitioner's bad behaviour, which amounted to a breach of fiduciary duty on his part, did not prevent him from succeeding with a claim for unfair prejudice.

<u>What was the background?</u>

The petitioner (Dr Potiamos) was the director of a software development company. A dispute arose with the company in relation to intellectual property rights in the software. The company brought a claim against Dr Potiamos who also petitioned under s.994 on the basis of exclusion from the management of the company.

<u>What did the court decide?</u>

The Judge at first instance decided that there was merit in the company's claim in relation to the software, and Dr Potamianos was ordered to hand it over, but also that there was unfair prejudice against Dr Potamianos and he should be bought out at a fair (undiscounted) value. The company appealed the judgment on various grounds.

On appeal counsel for the company (Mr Prescott), advanced a detailed case in support of the contention that the actions of Dr Potamianos, which were held to be a breach of fiduciary duty on his part, had justified his exclusion from management in what was held to be a quasi-partnership company. Various cases were cited in support of the contention that such behaviour justified exclusion. The Court of Appeal was robust in response to this and put it as follows:

> *"We do not consider that any of those cases undermine the judge's assessment of the overall position in this case. All concerned different types of misconduct/breaches of duty, and some were much more serious involving, e.g. dishonesty (including forgery and theft), bribery, secret negotiation with a competitor or diverting business to a rival. All involved secretive and/or dishonest conduct. Here, as already mentioned, Dr Potamianos engaged in an open and bona fide dispute as to ownership of certain intellectual property rights. The position that he took was ultimately held to have been wrong and he was found to have acted at one stage in the development of the dispute in a way that was unhelpful, evasive and in breach of his fiduciary duty to SEL. Ms Page accepted, however, as she was bound to do, that there is no rule of law that every breach of fiduciary duty will necessarily render exclusion from management fair: it is always a question of fact and degree. To show that a different conclusion was reached on the materially different facts of other cases does not advance Mr Prescott's case."*

The Court of Appeal also confirmed that the Judge was entitled to find that the purchase of Dr Potamianos' shares should be purchased without a discount. The case of *Re. Blue Index Limited [214] EWHC 2680 (Ch)* being specifically referred to in this context (see chapter 12).

The Sprintroom case reinforces that whilst there is a vast body of underlying case law, the court will ultimately assess cases on their own facts. Each side may find a raft of cases for and against a particular argument but these will only ever be part of the jigsaw when it comes to the Judge's decision. This means that there is an inherent degree of uncertainty as to outcome in most family business disputes, which do tend to be six of one and half dozen of the other when it comes to bad behaviour. This is one reason why litigation should always be considered the last resort in such disputes.

Dinglis v Dinglis – bad behaviour, not a quasi-partnership but still unfairly prejudiced

The case of *Re. Dinglis Properties Ltd [2019] EWHC 1664 (Ch)* is another example of a case where bad behaviour on the part of the petitioner did not preclude them from gaining a remedy.

What was the background?

This was a family property business, the son being given a 12% stake by his father. He eventually became sole director of the main company. Relationships between father and son soured dramatically and the father used his power as majority shareholder to remove the son as director of the main company. There were subsequently allegations that the son had wrongfully taken a large sum of money from a subsidiary company to fund a lavish lifestyle. Those allegations were later upheld.

The son then petitioned under s.994 claiming that he had been unfairly ejected from the company which he asserted was a quasi-partnership. His case was that there was a mutual understanding that the company would be run for the benefit of the family and that he would have the key role in running it. His removal from the company was accordingly a breach of this understanding and therefore unfair.

What did the court decide?

It was held that the company was not a quasi-partnership. The understandings relied on by the son were not found to exist and/or they were not capable of being relied on by the son. On that basis his exclusion from the business was not unfair. In summary, the court did not find that the father had relinquished control over the company to his son to the extent that he was alleging.

However, unfair prejudice was found as a result of the father making certain payments out of the company himself, in breach of his fiduciary duties. Had he not done so then it is likely that the son's petition would have failed completely, a clear lesson for majority shareholders in this situation.

With regard to the argument put forward by the father that the son's misconduct meant that he should not be granted relief, this was upheld in relation to the unfair prejudice arising from the son's dismissal as director. In this context it was confirmed that the court could take into account things which came to light after the dismissal in order to assess whether it was fair.

Such wrongdoing by the son was not however held to bar him from a remedy in relation to the unfair prejudice caused by the father's breach of fiduciary duties. Accordingly the court ordered that the father's holding company should purchase the son's shares. This was to be at a discounted rate to reflect the overall justice of the case.

A key point to take away from this case is that not all family companies will be quasi-partnerships. It is always going to depend on the facts of the case. A party claiming a legitimate expectation of an entitlement to a management role must evidence where that entitlement comes from. The mere fact that they have managed the business with relatively little interference from the majority shareholders is not enough, on its own, to justify displacing the majority shareholders legal rights to remove them.

CHAPTER FIFTEEN

CONCLUSIONS

Family companies are just like other companies but also very different. Disputes between shareholders in family businesses can require a subtly different approach in order to achieve successful resolution.

The underlying law and processes relevant to resolving internal disputes in family businesses are the same but the human element means that such disputes can be more bitter, more complex and more difficult to resolve. Recognising this difference is the first step in putting together a strategy to resolve the dispute.

Another key step is to really understand the cause of the dispute. Like arguments between married couples, what is being argued about may not actually be the cause of the argument. It may be the external expression of something deeper and identifying what this is can be an important factor in being able to reach a settlement. This is particularly the case if the dispute is ultimately mediated. Deals are done at mediation based as much on emotion and feelings as on the legal risk analysis.

There is a quote attributed to Maya Angelou which is pertinent in this respect:

> *"I've learned that people will forget what you said, people will forget what you did, but people will never forget how you made them feel."*

People will struggle to accept a deal or compromise, no matter how strongly the legal or commercial risk analysis favours acceptance, if they feel that it is unfair.

Furthermore, a feeling of unfairness retained from childhood can bubble up in shareholder disputes and mean that perceptions of later events are coloured on all sides and things blown out of proportion. It must be kept at the forefront of the adviser's mind that what determines whether something is "unfair" in a legal sense is not how the person feels about it but rather an objective assessment of all the circumstances.

Another required step is therefore to understand the factual context of the dispute. A dispute between shareholders is often essentially about two sides of the same story. Each side has their own narrative interpreting and making sense of what has happened. People involved in family disputes are more prone to creating a rigid (and sometimes highly subjective) personal narrative about what has happened because of the underlying emotional history that is involved. These narratives can be very convincing but must be reality tested. The role of a lawyer should include this reality testing and in particular an early assessment of the available documentation to see whether it supports, is adverse to, or merely neutral in relation to, the narrative being put forward.

One of the most important aspects of the factual background, which can sometimes be neglected by lawyers, whose natural affinity is often words rather than numbers, is the value of the shares in dispute. An objective assessment of value should be sought at an early stage. This enables a proper assessment of the commerciality of any strategy to be assessed. There is generally no commercial rationale for spending hundreds of thousands of legal fees to pursue a case involving shares worth tens of thousands. A client may wish to pursue a case as a "point of principle" but experience suggests that this rarely ends well.

A further step is to reflect upon the particular issues which arise depending upon whether you are on the majority side or the minority side. Awareness of these issues, and anticipating how they may arise in the context of any particular dispute, will help in creating a successful strategy.

Once the context has been fully established then the step of carrying out a legal analysis can be most effectively undertaken. This analysis does require some experience in order to be done properly. Both s.994 and s.122(1)(g) are short sections in very long Acts but underpinning them are decades of case law. In addition to this there are aspects of the procedure that can also amount to elephant traps for the unwary.

On that basis the legal adviser should be prepared to get expert advice unless they are confident they have this expertise themselves. Getting an expert counsel (barrister) involved at an early stage can be invaluable.

This can be particularly important in family business disputes where solicitors, by virtue of their often close relationships with their clients can risk being drawn into a particular narrative and then cease to see the wood for the trees. Experienced counsel, acting as a second pair of eyes, can be an important part of the reality testing process.

That reality testing process is also essential in terms of analysing offers of settlement, whether and when to make them, and how to respond to those received. Offers made in shareholders disputes can have more significant consequences than in standard litigation and need to be objectively analysed.

Finally, it should be understood that litigation is a very blunt tool to try and resolve a matter as complex as a shareholder dispute within a family business. Whilst some may believe that the high emotions involved militate against using techniques such as mediation to resolve these disputes, experience suggests that the opposite is true. Mediation can provide a forum to ventilate the underlying issues giving rise to the conflict and its flexibility makes it a powerful tool to achieve settlement.

Following these steps should maximise the chances of successfully resolving any shareholders dispute but like families each dispute is different and what works in one will fall flat in another. To quote the first sentence of Anna Karenina by Leo Tolstoy:

> *"Happy families are all alike; every unhappy family is unhappy in its own way"*

The hope is that this book will have given some useful signposts and tools to help advisers of family businesses that are in dispute to guide those unhappy families to find the route to a resolution.

MORE BOOKS BY LAW BRIEF PUBLISHING

'Covid-19, Homeworking and the Law – The Essential Guide to Employment and GDPR Issues' by Forbes Solicitors
'Covid-19, Force Majeure and Frustration of Contracts – The Essential Guide' by Keith Markham
'Covid-19 and Criminal Law – The Essential Guide' by Ramya Nagesh
'Covid-19 and Family Law in England and Wales – The Essential Guide' by Safda Mahmood
'A Practical Guide to the Law of Unlawful Eviction and Harassment – 2nd Edition' by Stephanie Lovegrove
'Covid-19, Residential Property, Equity Release and Enfranchisement – The Essential Guide' by Paul Sams and Louise Uphill
'Covid-19, Brexit and the Law of Commercial Leases – The Essential Guide' by Mark Shelton
'A Practical Guide to Costs in Personal Injury Claims – 2nd Edition' by Matthew Hoe
'A Practical Guide to the General Data Protection Regulation (GDPR) – 2nd Edition' by Keith Markham
'Ellis on Credit Hire – Sixth Edition' by Aidan Ellis & Tim Kevan
'A Practical Guide to Working with Litigants in Person and McKenzie Friends in Family Cases' by Stuart Barlow
'Protecting Unregistered Brands: A Practical Guide to the Law of Passing Off' by Lorna Brazell
'A Practical Guide to Secondary Liability and Joint Enterprise Post-Jogee' by Joanne Cecil & James Mehigan
'A Practical Guide to the Pre-Action RTA Claims Protocol for Personal Injury Lawyers' by Antonia Ford
'A Practical Guide to Neighbour Disputes and the Law' by Alexander Walsh
'A Practical Guide to Forfeiture of Leases' by Mark Shelton
'A Practical Guide to Coercive Control for Legal Practitioners and Victims' by Rachel Horman

'A Practical Guide to Rights Over Airspace and Subsoil' by Daniel Gatty
'Tackling Disclosure in the Criminal Courts – A Practitioner's Guide' by Narita Bahra QC & Don Ramble
'A Practical Guide to the Law of Driverless Cars – Second Edition' by Alex Glassbrook, Emma Northey & Scarlett Milligan
'A Practical Guide to TOLATA Claims' by Greg Williams
'Artificial Intelligence – The Practical Legal Issues' by John Buyers
'A Practical Guide to the Law of Prescription in Scotland' by Andrew Foyle
'A Practical Guide to the Construction and Rectification of Wills and Trust Instruments' by Edward Hewitt
'A Practical Guide to the Law of Bullying and Harassment in the Workplace' by Philip Hyland
'How to Be a Freelance Solicitor: A Practical Guide to the SRA-Regulated Freelance Solicitor Model' by Paul Bennett
'A Practical Guide to Prison Injury Claims' by Malcolm Johnson
'A Practical Guide to the Small Claims Track' by Dominic Bright
'A Practical Guide to Advising Clients at the Police Station' by Colin Stephen McKeown-Beaumont
'A Practical Guide to Antisocial Behaviour Injunctions' by Iain Wightwick
'Practical Mediation: A Guide for Mediators, Advocates, Advisers, Lawyers, and Students in Civil, Commercial, Business, Property, Workplace, and Employment Cases' by Jonathan Dingle with John Sephton
'The Mini-Pupillage Workbook' by David Boyle
'A Practical Guide to Crofting Law' by Brian Inkster
'A Practical Guide to Spousal Maintenance' by Liz Cowell
'A Practical Guide to the Law of Domain Names and Cybersquatting' by Andrew Clemson
'A Practical Guide to the Law of Gender Pay Gap Reporting' by Harini Iyengar

'A Practical Guide to the Rights of Grandparents in Children Proceedings' by Stuart Barlow

'NHS Whistleblowing and the Law' by Joseph England

'Employment Law and the Gig Economy' by Nigel Mackay & Annie Powell

'A Practical Guide to Noise Induced Hearing Loss (NIHL) Claims' by Andrew Mckie, Ian Skeate, Gareth McAloon

'An Introduction to Beauty Negligence Claims – A Practical Guide for the Personal Injury Practitioner' by Greg Almond

'Intercompany Agreements for Transfer Pricing Compliance' by Paul Sutton

'Zen and the Art of Mediation' by Martin Plowman

'A Practical Guide to the SRA Principles, Individual and Law Firm Codes of Conduct 2019 – What Every Law Firm Needs to Know' by Paul Bennett

'A Practical Guide to Adoption for Family Lawyers' by Graham Pegg

'A Practical Guide to Industrial Disease Claims' by Andrew Mckie & Ian Skeate

'A Practical Guide to Redundancy' by Philip Hyland

'A Practical Guide to Vicarious Liability' by Mariel Irvine

'A Practical Guide to Applications for Landlord's Consent and Variation of Leases' by Mark Shelton

'A Practical Guide to Relief from Sanctions Post-Mitchell and Denton' by Peter Causton

'A Practical Guide to Equity Release for Advisors' by Paul Sams

'A Practical Guide to the Law Relating to Food' by Ian Thomas

'A Practical Guide to Financial Services Claims' by Chris Hegarty

'The Law of Houses in Multiple Occupation: A Practical Guide to HMO Proceedings' by Julian Hunt

'A Practical Guide to Unlawful Eviction and Harassment' by Stephanie Lovegrove

'Occupiers, Highways and Defective Premises Claims: A Practical Guide Post-Jackson – 2nd Edition' by Andrew Mckie

www.ingramcontent.com/pod-product-compliance
Lightning Source LLC
LaVergne TN
LVHW022058200926
848481LV00003B/975